HUMANIZING LEADERSHIP

Reflection Fuels
People Matter
Relationships Make the Difference

HUGH MACLEOD

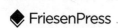 FriesenPress

Suite 300 - 990 Fort St
Victoria, BC, V8V 3K2
Canada

www.friesenpress.com

ISBN
978-1-5255-2718-0 (Hardcover)
978-1-5255-2719-7 (Paperback)
978-1-5255-2720-3 (eBook)

1. Self-Help

Distributed to the trade by The Ingram Book Company

TABLE OF CONTENTS

CHAPTER I
WHAT MOST LEADERSHIP CONVERSATIONS GLOSS OVER

CHAPTER II
ARE HEARTS, SPIRITS AND MINDS IMPORTANT TO YOU?

CHAPTER III
ORGANIZATIONAL ELASTICITY AND EFFECTIVENESS

CHAPTER IV
PARADOX OF SIMULTANEOUS CONTINUITY AND CHANGE

CHAPTER V
ADAPTIVE ACTION AND LEADERSHIP

CHAPTER VI
CHOOSE NOT TO MIMIC LEADERSHIP PERSONAS

Cultivate Humanizing Leadership

Plant this seed within your core
Provide it space to sprout, and tend to its rise
Ensure it penetrates through each organizational layer
Cultivation, participation, and appreciation will be your essential tools
Allow this seed to transform into a solid footing
A personal and organizational launch pad
This mighty seed has significant yield
A vigorous and holistic whole

WHY I WROTE THIS BOOK

I have been working on this book throughout my personal and professional life. I am interested in the connection between personal and reflective learning and the power of healthy relationship patterns.

From my experience, few people are burdened by self-awareness. When I held up a mirror to my people interactions I realized something: Who is always there? It's me, and I noticed myself engaging in relationship patterns over and over again with different people.

This book will change the way you look at leadership and at yourself. It strives to have you hold a mirror up to your beliefs about who you are, and leadership in general, to help you discover what sort of leader you were naturally destined to be.

For better or worse, we have deeply developed characteristics and tendencies within us. If we are honest with ourselves, we acknowledge our own habits, preferences, and understandings that are difficult, if not impossible, for others to break or alter.

As a student of leadership studies my personal library is filled with leadership books and articles. Many of these publications outline, from the author's lens, the necessary attributes required to fit a preconceived leadership mold.

This book is not a leadership guide. It's not a leadership 101 class set to dictate the definition of leadership. This book is aimed at leadership configuration, and how we create and cultivate our own unique leadership form. Through forty-two leadership vignettes, the book examines held leadership beliefs and what triggers emotional reaction, thought and reflection.

While this book uses a volume of leadership science authored by academics to anchor principles and concepts, paired with anecdotal insights and perspective garnered through personal and professional experiences, it should be treated as an instrument for creating dialogue and discussion and formulating the necessary questions to put your own leadership assumptions to the test.

To emerging leaders not yet armoured against the craziness of context, *Humanizing Leadership* examines the various aspects of leadership, while putting an emphasis on the individual's need to become his or her own style of leader through in-depth self-examination, rather than trying to mimic the style of others.

The pages that follow examine how reflection fuels, people matter, and relationships make a difference. These three threads are used to weave a tapestry of self-discovery and personal growth.

The book will help you see what is in you and in front of you!

HOW TO USE THIS BOOK

This book requires reader participation. The weight of the message is within the reader, not on the pages.

The book provides an opportunity to test personal assumptions, reasoning, and orientation. It would be a grave mistake to think it could generate the same questions and insights in everyone. Each person will interact with this book differently and obtain their personal understandings regardless of the fixed framework and content provided. People will gain from this book what they are prepared to reflect on and see. The questions we ask ourselves, the obstacles we face, the experiences we have been subjected to, and our personal understandings personalize our interpretations and interactions.

The words and ideas shared here are by no means universal truths. They are personal experiences and understandings that are open to adaptation. Use the personal insights as a springboard for self-discovery. Note the pages or insights that encourage your self-reflection. Mark the lines or sections that challenge your views. Revisit these inclinations at a later date to determine whether their weight or significance is lasting.

While reading, notice what personal truths arise within you and persistently call for further consideration. Allow your epiphanies and frustrations to emerge, understand the congestion that hampers, and the possibilities that extend your leadership growth. Interact with this book at a pace, and in a method, that suits your individual style.

A reviewer offered this reaction to the instructions… "I can be a little bit jaded, I didn't really believe that those instructions would actually prove useful. But having read the book now, I can definitely see the value in that approach—using this not as a book to read and put down or shelve forever, but a resource to keep returning to, to be able to take small nuggets at a time as needed, to use it to assess your own changing reactions over time and in different situations."

This book is presented as a learning tool, and therefore, the goal is to provide prompts for your leadership exploration. Throughout the book there will be invites for your reflection.

There is no right way, other than forward.

Your journey begins!

ABOUT THE AUTHOR

Over his working career, Hugh had the privilege of experiencing many organizational environments: retail sales; ownership of a small business; human-resource-management services in the insurance, utility, and healthcare sectors; labour relations and labour negotiations; board governance and advisory work; learner engagement at various universities; local and provincial healthcare administration; government service; provincial climate-change planning; and national quality and safety improvement.

He's spent time as front-line worker, middle manager, senior executive, and chief operating officer. In the process, he has gained an appreciation of the dynamics that take place between people and relationships within and between organizational spaces.

His executive leadership experience includes: senior vice president, Health Employers Association of BC; senior vice president and interim CEO, Vancouver Coastal-Health Authority; assistant deputy minister, Ontario Ministry of Health and Long-Term Care; associate deputy minister and executive lead of Ontario's Health Results Team; associate deputy minister, Climate Change Ontario Government Cabinet Office, and CEO, Canadian Patient Safety Institute.

In addition to professional accomplishments, Hugh is a consummate learner and knowledge-exchange advocate and lecturer. Professional activities have included: adjunct professor at Griffith University Business School in Brisbane, Australia and senior fellow at the University of Toronto, Rotman School of Management. Currently an adjunct professor for the School of Population and Public Health at the University of British Columbia, Hugh greatly cherishes the teaching environment and the profound unveilings it brings forth.

As a sought-after speaker on leadership and transformational strategy, he pushes tenaciously to establish new narratives pertaining to change, transformation, and leadership. Current assumptions and theories are often employed well beyond their intended purpose, scope, and/or means. As such, Hugh continually pushes to extend conversations beyond their present standing and bring forth new ways of thinking.

Being an enthusiast of leadership writings, Hugh chose to harness the power of the written word to further his learning message. He uses writing as a tool to uncover and establish new understandings within himself while providing others with a new way of seeing. The motivating factor behind his writing is to increase the number of minds and voices that can participate in the process of change and transformation. Writing provides Hugh with a platform to explore, reflect, and challenge personal assumptions while inciting new possibilities.

Hugh is eternally grateful for the multitude of individuals who graciously shared their time, words, wisdom, and encouragement with him along his leadership journey. Often, these individuals had confidence in him before he had confidence in his own ability. These individuals provided him with the essential space and pivotal opportunities to grow.

His enthusiasm is derived from his desire to facilitate change and be of service to future leaders, and to give back, extending to them the same generosities that were bestowed upon him.

CHAPTER I
WHAT MOST LEADERSHIP CONVERSATIONS GLOSS OVER

*"Being a leader does not require a title; having
a title does not make you one."*
~ *Unknown*

INTRODUCTION

Understanding "self" through reflection is a key foundation for cultivating humanizing leadership. Every leader is unique. We all stem from our own circumstance. The South African poet Machado said, "The road is your footsteps, nothing else." It is your sole responsibility to determine how to proceed along your personal path. The only obstacle obstructing your leadership quest is self. The extent of your leadership growth is contingent on your own commitment, courage, and fervour.

In this chapter I begin a conversation about what makes leadership personal and hard. This is followed by definitions of leadership and the importance of drafting your personal leadership definition. There is an acknowledgement that leadership development cannot be imposed, and I share a number of leadership development traps that I fell into on my personal leadership journey. This leads to a conversation about our human hard drives that contain biases, virus experiences, blind spots, and coping mechanisms. A discussion about organizational truths and untruths creates an important foundation for a short dive into three organizational space conditions. I end with a paradox; everyone wants to change and no one wants to change.

We would not set out to reproduce the masterpiece *Birth of Venus* just because we were given the same brushes, palette, and a step-by-step guide. Yes, leadership tools and frameworks are important, but self-development and understanding are vital.

LEADERSHIP IS PERSONAL

Twenty-eight years ago, renowned management and leadership expert Peter Drucker made a back-to-the-future prediction: "In a few hundred years, when the history of our time will be written from a long-term perspective, it is likely that the most important event historians will see is not technology, not the internet, not e-commerce. It is an unprecedented change in the human condition. For the first time, literally substantial and rapidly growing numbers of people have choices. For the first time, they will have to manage themselves. And society is totally unprepared for it."[1]

Given that you purchased this book, I assume the following: You are interested in leadership, you have read countless words about leadership and perhaps attended a course or conference on the topic, and you are a leader. There's something you need to know: Most leadership books, leadership conferences, and workshops gloss over (or avoid altogether) the fact that leadership is personal, very hard work, and on everyone's mind!

Pick up the newspaper, watch the daily news, search the Internet; leadership (or lack thereof) is a hot topic everywhere. Today, political, private, and public-sector leadership is on everyone's mind and has never played a more prominent role in international, national, and local conversations. Private sector leaders are often seen as financially motivated personally—some to the point of being corrupt. Public sector leaders are often portrayed as incompetent. Levels of trust in politicians and government are constantly under public and media scrutiny. Ideological debates about organizations often dominate newspaper pages, while concrete and proven strategies for improving organizational performance receive little or no attention. Leaders visit renowned centres of excellence around the world and return full of enthusiasm for change. Yet many organizational terrains are extremely rigid and presided over by powerful top-down players—a landscape where every inch of organizational boundary space is hotly contested.

We have library shelves stacked with research studies, books, articles, and papers on organizational leadership and transformation, and inboxes with course and workshop materials from the leadership development and transformation industry. We have boardrooms with transformative ideas. We have leadership-change conferences, and symposiums filled with brilliant minds. We receive improvement insights from front-line workers and customer experiences, sign contracts with consultants for analysis, and have tools to improve organizational performance.

So why is it so difficult to have performance improvement in spite of the availability of all this firepower, requisite skills, influence, and determination? In 2013 Peter Bergen, in his article "Why So Many Leadership Programs Ultimately Fail." suggests: What makes leadership personal and hard work isn't the theoretical; it's the practical. It's not about knowing what to say or do. It's about whether you're willing to experience the discomfort, risk, and uncertainty of saying or doing it. To quote Aristotle, "To avoid discomfort, say nothing, do nothing, be nothing."[2]

On avoiding discomfort, Bergen offers: "The critical challenge of leadership is, mostly the challenge of emotional courage. Emotional courage means standing apart from others without separating yourself from them. It means speaking up when others are silent. And remaining steadfast, grounded, and measured in the face of uncertainty. It means responding to political opposition and games without getting sidetracked, distracted, or losing your focus. And staying in the discomfort without shutting off or becoming defensive."[3]

Laurent Ledoux posed a very important leadership question in a 2009 synthesis of the Practice of Adaptive Leadership. "If leadership involves will and skill, does it also require the engagement of all of you: mind, spirit, heart, and guts?"[4] Isabel Ramos in a 2006 research paper titled "The Organizational Mindset" makes the point that "terms such as knowledge management, organizational memory and business intelligence and organizational learning are becoming usual in social and leadership discourse." [5] She goes on to suggest "each presupposes a parallel between the individual human mind, spirit, heart, and guts and the organizational capability of the collective organizational mind, spirit, heart, and guts to support the planning and execution of new and better solutions to problems and opportunities." [5]

Skill requires learning new competencies, with your mind training your body to become proficient at understanding and practicing, every day, the reality that reflection fuels, people matter, and relationships make the difference. In 2006, Peter Senge, author and founder of the Society for Organizational Learning, was asked a penetrating question about will and skill: "Are the basic fundamentals for sound leadership the same, and are we just responding to a different world or are we fundamentally shifting?" He responded: "For me, the fundamentals start with a set of deep capacities with which few in leadership positions today could claim to have developed: environmental intelligence, building relationships across boundaries and openness of mind, heart and will. To develop such capacities requires a lifelong commitment to grow as a human being in ways not well understood in contemporary culture. Yet, in other ways, these are fundamentals for leadership that have been understood for a very long time. Unfortunately, this ancient knowledge has been largely lost in the modern era of quick fix." [6]

In 2015, Jeffrey Pfeffer, in his book *Leadership BS,* suggests: "The problem with leadership is at its core a story of disconnections: the disconnect between what leaders say and what they do; the disconnect between the leadership industry's prescriptions and the reality of many leaders' behaviors and traits; the disconnect between the multidimensional nature of leadership performance and the simple, non-contingent answers so many people seek; the disconnect between how the leadership industry is evaluated (happy sheets that tap inspiration and satisfaction) and the actual consequences of leader failures (miserable workplaces and career derailments); the disconnect between leader performance and behavior and the consequences those leaders face; the disconnect between what most people seem to want (good news, nice stories, emotional uplift) and what they need (the truth); the disconnect between what would make workplaces better and organizations more effective, and the base rate with which such prescriptions get implemented."[7]

The views of Senge and Pfeffer were captured much earlier in a 1999 CBC interview with respected Canadian management expert Henry Mintzberg, in which he made the following observation on what he calls capital "L" leadership behaviour, as opposed to what he calls small-letter leadership behaviour. "Capital 'L' has made society unmanageable and poses grave dangers. By small-letter leadership, I simply mean that natural practice of leadership in very human and connected ways. That's not posing a threat … that's necessary. I think the thing that's posing a threat is the big capital-letter leadership, which is all the formality, labelling, titling, techniques, status, image, and phoniness … the whole approach to leadership that's based on people who are disconnected from what they manage and a cult of leadership in which the organization exists for the leaders.

"We don't know where the hell the organization is heading, but everything has to be shaken up. When you see the list of capabilities and competencies of what it takes to be a good leader, Superman's abilities are modest in comparison. We list everything imaginable … I think really good leaders are tremendously candid … They're very honest and open … People who are insecure play everything close to the hilt, use knowledge and theory as a basis of power … Organizations exist for their products and services supplied to their customers … They do not exist for their leaders and managers. We live in a cult of leadership, in which the organization exists for the leaders … It's a pecking order of who's got the power and who sits in what relationship to the chief executive … It's all very silly, really."[8]

Here's my take away: You need to personalize leadership and be authentic. Don't give and speak the leadership mumbo jumbo. Make it your own and express it in your own way. Many people go out of their way to try to be a leader, but they have no idea why; their leadership ideas are straight out of books, and they don't know how to connect with people. They operate as leadership theorists. As Kouzes and Posner put it: "Leadership is an art, a performing art, and the instrument is self."[9]

The idea that the instrument for leadership is self, reminds me of the story of Konosuke Matsushita, born the youngest of eight children in a rice famer's family. An apprentice at age nine, by twenty-two he owned his own business, Matsushita Electrical Appliance Factory, which was built on the idea of a better electrical socket. It now produces products known by the names Panasonic, Technics, Quasar, and many others such as the batteries for Tesla cars.

Matsushita spoke often about his philosophy of business and leadership. Leadership expert and author John Kotter captured his leadership philosophy in the book: *Matsushita Leadership*. For the purposes of my book, I selected Matsushita's philosophy about employees: "There are several ways of leading and managing one's employees. One, apparently, is to use extraordinary wisdom and exert charismatic leadership in order to inspire workers to do their best. I have never approached my job that way, since lacking in both those qualities; I do not belong in this category of leader. I am the type who consults his staff and asks for their wisdom. If I have a secret, it is a natural inclination to trust my staff and seek their cooperation. I trust my employees for what they know and what they have done."[10]

The quest for leadership is an inner quest to discover who you are and what you care about, and it's through this process of self-examination that you find the awareness needed to lead. Think about people who you view as being great leaders. Reflect on whether or not you believe they accepted responsibility to develop and express their own unique vision, purpose, and values.

It's when we examine our lives that we are able to identify the changes we need to make to develop and humanize our leadership. Until we truly know ourselves, our strengths and weaknesses, what we want to do, and why we want to do it, we can only succeed in the most superficial sense of the word.

People like to follow genuine people whose whole mind and soul goes into leading and making everyone around them better. People want to be able to relate to their leaders and have a relationship to know they are real. Who wants to follow a copycat? Who wants to be a copycat? Be someone so unique that others around you want to follow you because you are real.

Where are you experiencing leadership discomfort, risk, and uncertainty? Is your leadership journey connected with your interior self?

DEFINE YOUR LEADERSHIP

One ship sails east and another sails west,
With the self same winds that blow;
'Tis the set of the sails and not the gales
That tells them where to go.

Like the winds of the sea are the winds of time,
As we journey along through life;
'Tis the set of the soul that determines the goal,
And not the calm or the strife.
~Ella Wheeler Wilcox, 1916

If our sails are set correctly, our personal leadership philosophy, not the gales we encounter every day will tell us where to go. In 2018 D. Benson, in his article "How To Determine Your Personal Leadership Philosophy," offers the following insights: "One of the most important things you can do to become effective leaders is to think about, define and then articulate your own personal leadership philosophy. Here are three reasons why it can become the key to your effectiveness."[11]

1. YOUR CONSISTENCY

"Your personal leadership philosophy gives you consistency. Without a leadership philosophy, your actions and your reactions will reflect the tensions of the moment.

2. YOUR TRUE NORTH

Your leadership philosophy becomes your true north. Everything you do, everything you say, every action, every decision, every plan is filtered through your philosophy.

3. YOUR PERSONAL MISSION

Your philosophy is all about your own personal mission and who you are as a leader. If you are not clear on your personal mission, your role as a leader will not be clear."[11]

Successful organizations have a personal compelling vision and mission wrapped in values, and they develop strategies to inspire people to use their talents to meet organizational goals for improved business results. Leading yourself means applying these same principles to your role as a leader. Personal leadership does not just make for better business; it makes for better leadership. It makes for a better you.

If you look up "leadership definitions" in a Google search, in .44 seconds you will get over 243,000,000 results. The Google search of leadership definitions show there are as many definitions as there are leaders. This is a good thing, because it recognizes that leadership is deeply personal and a topic to be wrestled with by each of us as we prepare to lead.

The following leadership definitions speak to five themes: influence, change, service, character, and development. The definitions are from the Internet provider "Brainy Quote." You will notice from this collection, there is no one single definition of leadership.

Leadership as Influence

"Leadership is influence–nothing more, nothing less."
– J. Maxwell, *The 21 Irrefutable Laws of Leadership*

"Leadership is the art of influencing others to their maximum performance to accomplish any task, objective or project."
– W. Cohen, *The Art of a Leader*

"Leadership is the process of influencing the activities of an individual or a group in efforts toward goal achievement in a given situation." – H. P. Hershey, K. Blanchard, D. Johnson, *Management of Organizational Behaviour*

Leadership as Change

"Leadership defines what the future should look like, aligns people with that vision, and inspires them to make it happen despite the obstacles." – J. Kotter, *Leading Change*

"Leadership is the art of mobilizing others to want to struggle for shared aspirations." – J. M. Kouzes and B. Z. Posner, *The Leadership Challenge*

"Leadership is the capacity of individuals to spark the capacity of a human community–people living and working together–to bring forth new realities." – P. Senge, *Fifth Discipline*

Leadership as Character

"Leadership is a combination of strategy and character. If you must be without one, be without the strategy." – General H. Schwarzkopf

"Leadership: The capacity and will to rally people to a common purpose together with the character that inspires confidence and trust" – Field Marshal Montgomery

"Leadership is not a person or a position. It is a complex moral relationship between people, based on trust, obligation, commitment, emotion, and a shared vision of the good." – J. Ciulla, *Leadership at the Crossroads*

Leadership as Service

"Leadership is about service to others and a commitment to developing more servants as leaders. It involves co-creation of a commitment to a mission." – R. Greenleaf, *The Power of Servant Leadership*

"The first responsibility of a leader is to define reality. The last is to say thank you. In between the two, the leader must become a servant and a debtor. That sums up the progress of an artful leader." – M. DePree, *Leadership Art*

"All of the great leaders have had one characteristic in common: It was the willingness to confront unequivocally the major anxiety of their people in their time. This, and not much else, is the essence of leadership." – J. K. Galbraith, *The New Industrial State.*

Stephen R. Covey introduced the concept of a personal leadership statement in *The 7 Habits of Highly Effective People*. In the second habit, 'Begin with the End in Mind', Covey argues everything is created twice, once in our imagination, as we visualize an outcome, and again when we actually achieve the goal. A personal leadership statement that draws on your values and desired end-goal helps integrate this thinking into your life.

Creating a personal mission and vision statement is important because it's easy to get distracted, to lose sight of what's important to us. When we get disconnected from our direction, other people's agendas come before our own. Have you noticed how, at times, every phone call, email, and notification on your screen draws your full attention? While at other times, you're absorbed in your work regardless of the distraction? Your personal mission and vision doesn't eliminate distraction. It inspires us to focus on what matters. It provides clarity for the future while directing us to place our attention in the present.

Creating my personal and living definition of leadership affected how I thought about my roles, choices made, how I acted, my relationship with others, and ultimately, personal and organizational results. As I began to immerse myself in the narrative of my personal leadership definition, I found myself questioning and challenging my perspective on long-held beliefs and views. A transformation occurred as I reflected, and it moved me to reframe my own thinking, it helped me explore and discover my inner edge.

Joelle Jay in the book *The Inner Edge: The 10 Practices of Personal Leadership*, shares important insights about the need to periodically turn away from the concerns of the day – the people, the problems and the pressure – to explore and discover your inner edge. "To practice personal leadership, you apply the principles of leadership that make businesses a success to yourself. For example, leading in business involves having a compelling vision, developing strategies and inspiring people to use their talents to meet a goal for improved business results. Leading yourself means applying these same principles of leadership to your role as a leader and your life. You, too, need a compelling vision and a strategy for reaching it. You need a team supporting you. You need results, as well as a sense of contribution and purpose.[12]

In summary Joelle Jay suggests 10 practices of personal leadership: Get clarity, find your focus, take action, tap into your brilliance, feel fulfillment, maximize your time, build your team, keep learning, see possibility, and all at once. So now the key question is, are you succeeding in leading yourself? Take the following quiz developed by Joelle Jay [12] to find out.

Personal Leadership Quiz
Answer each of the following questions with a
"yes," "sometimes," or "no" response.

1. I am clear on what I want and know how to get it – for the big things and the small. Yes Sometimes No

2. I practice a strategic, reflective approach to leadership. Yes Sometimes No

---

3. I know where to focus my attention on a daily basis.
Yes Sometimes No

4. I am able to maintain peak performance at all times.
Yes Sometimes No

5. I maintain my sense of stability and equilibrium in times of change. Yes Sometimes No

6. I have identified my talents, strengths, skills, and weaknesses. Yes Sometimes No

7. I know how to maximize and leverage my unique talents and abilities. Yes Sometimes No

8. I am delighted with my quality of life both on and off the job. Yes Sometimes No

9. I feel very little stress and overwhelm in my life. Yes Sometimes No

10. I make a meaningful contribution every day. Yes Sometimes No

11. I have plenty of time for people, activities and events that are most important to me. Yes Sometimes No

12. I take regular action toward my most important goals – not just what's most pressing. Yes Sometimes No

13. I have a wide network of people who support me, and whom I support in return. Yes Sometimes No

14. I am constantly learning and improving myself. Yes Sometimes No

15. I intuitively recognize and take opportunities. Yes Sometimes No

16. I am often astounded by the way the opportunities I want and the solutions I need present themselves at just the right moment. Yes Sometimes No

17. I achieve a sense of renewal and restoration on a daily basis. Yes Sometimes No

18. I am proud of my ability to maintain my values and the essence of who I am, even when life gets hectic and/or as I get more and more responsibility. Yes Sometimes No

19. I have achieved "success" as I define it. Yes Sometimes No

20. I can say with confidence that every day I am at my very best. Yes Sometimes No

Your Score

"For each "yes" response, give yourself 2 points. For each "sometimes" response, give yourself 1 point. For each "no" response, give yourself 0 points.

What Your Score Means

0-13 points, you're likely new at personal leadership. You're so focused on the image you're putting out to the world that you're neglecting your personal leadership. Chances are you're doing what you've always done. As a result, you're not being very strategic about what you're doing and why. It's time to take a break from the action of business, go backstage, and do the inner work of who you are as a leader, what you want to contribute, and how you can find the ideal strategy for achieving what you want to achieve.

14-27 points. If you scored in the mid-range, you are spending some time on yourself, but you're not being strategic in terms of getting the right balance for yourself. You may often feel that both business and life are "hit or miss." You're getting some benefits, but you're not getting all the benefits you could. Therefore, look at where you're excelling. These are your strengths. Find a way to refine those strengths even more so you can capitalize on them better. Then, look at where you rated yourself low. Those are your weaknesses. Find a way to develop those areas so you get more power.

28-40 points. If your score is high, congratulations! You are very often thoughtful and strategic on what you're doing and why. Continue developing your skills.[12]

How are you developing your inner edge?

LEADERSHIP CANNOT
BE IMPOSED

When we think about who is going to be the next generation of leaders, we need to understand the environment they come from. From the time they were children, they were being involved in decisions from things as small as what they wanted to eat for dinner to things like where they wanted to go on the yearly family vacation. So, it is impossible to now put them in a work environment that does not include them in a decision-making framework at all levels.

Warren Bennis, pioneer of the contemporary field of leadership studies and referred to as the father of leadership, reinforced that leadership is personal and cannot be imposed: "No leader sets out to be a leader. People set out to live their lives, expressing themselves fully. When that expression is of value, they become leaders. So, the point is not to become a leader. The point is to become yourself, to use yourself completely—all your skills, gifts, and energies—in order to make your vision manifest. You must withhold nothing. You must, in sum, become the person you started out to be, and to enjoy the process of becoming... Leaders have nothing but themselves to work with... we are our own raw material. Only when we know what we're made of and what we want to make of it can we begin our lives and we must do it despite an unwitting conspiracy of people and events against us...To become a leader, then, you must become yourself, become the maker of your own life...Know thyself, then, means separating who you are and who you want to be from what the world thinks you are and wants you to be... Until you make your life your own, you're walking around in borrowed clothes."[13]

Building on the wisdom from Bennis, becoming a leader starts with knowing yourself and what you want to make of your life. Knowing yourself is the foundation of character, purpose, and authenticity. It's only when you understand who you are, not what the world thinks you are, that you're ready to lead. A starting point is asking, "What have I gotten myself into?" Doing that requires understanding and learning.

Learning is not an end in and of itself but a means to process our experiences, tune our versatility, and establish the necessary skills for life's constant shifts. Leadership knowledge, like all knowledge, is not limited or bound. Leadership knowledge demands perpetual growth and adaptation. The obstacles we face within ourselves, and the organizations we serve, must continually be outgrown. Learning requires us to be vulnerable, open to varying perspectives, and willing to test the validity of our beliefs and those held by others. It starts with our involvement, questioning, and curiosity, and followed by self-reflection.

As leaders we are aware of leadership studies, libraries filled with leadership books and articles offering up recipes for numerous advancements and outcomes; they are written, for the most part, from a tidy and linear lens. Nonetheless, we often select and apply these newly found, revisited, and updated frameworks to the pressing problems we face. Unfortunately, the promises found within these frameworks usually dissolve before the expected transformation can take hold. The knowledge and know-how at our disposal often remains inert because of our lack of self-understanding, the insufficient consideration of our people, and our failure to recognize organizational context and the impact relationships have on organizational productivity and workplace wellness. We eagerly return to the bookshelf searching for a different angle to implement change, hoping that this time it will penetrate and bring forth the intended result.

Dickson and Tholl, in *Bringing Leadership to Life In Health,* put it this way: "Learning leadership is different because the setting for leadership is almost always fluid and unpredictable, and there are factors at play in dynamic settings that can make learning a challenge." They go on to suggest that: "learning leadership must adapt to these factors: leadership is situational; effective leadership is in the eye of the follower; experience is both practical and emotional; growth happens through learning and unlearning; and learning leadership is a lifelong process."[14]

And what have I learned? Real-world experiences create real-world leadership. Without experience, we run the risk of creating leadership theorists versus leaders. Leadership is learned through trial and error, through mucking it up and making mistakes and having the gumption to learn from what worked and did not work.

Unfortunately, in our instant-microwave culture, we want to be leaders now! And we focus so much on trying to be a leader *now* that we forget that leadership is learned along the way and does not just happen overnight.

What word or words would you use to describe your personal leadership learning?

PERSONAL LEADERSHIP TRAPS

Do we fall into a trap of forcing from the top a blueprint, a plan, a process, a tool, without truly allowing for the generation of a new way of thinking and doing business? Not acknowledging this trap is one of the biggest personal leadership traps a leader can ever make.

Many leaders face complex organizational challenges that refuse to budge no matter how hard they and others work on them. They spend time, energy and resources to no avail. Tanya Menon and Leigh Thompson in their book *"Stop Spending, Start Managing,"* study this phenomenon of action without traction, when organizations, sometimes in frenzy, expend considerable effort to get nowhere.

From interviews with hundreds of leaders who failed to achieve their goals, they identified five systemic leadership traps: experience; winners; agreement; communications and macro-management. Each flow from strength that at times can turn into a flaw.

THE EXPERTISE TRAP

"Expertise has many attractive benefits, often allowing people to effortlessly exercise excellent judgment and achieve success. As experts in their domain, often leaders react automatically to many situations, essentially on autopilot. With their mind turned off, they can lose touch with their inner compass and narrow their thinking. Because you are so knowledgeable, you fall into predictable patterns and it's difficult to see how to break out of it.

THE WINNER'S TRAP

"Leaders and the people they work with are in their jobs through winning the interview, getting promoted, and are often reluctant to jeopardize their situation by losing. Sometimes we are so focused on winning, we lose the big picture. We're competing, not co-operating. We forsake our values. The competition and or rival who might help, is shut out of conversations and strategies to solve departmental and organizational issues. In addition, in many organizations, people get trapped in a fruitless course of action because staying the course is rewarded, whereas failing, learning, and accepting losses are not. We continue investing time and resources to projects we sense have failed, because of a reluctance to admit failure.

THE AGREEMENT TRAP

"Rather than speaking honestly and confronting problems head-on, those caught in the agreement trap are overly concerned with being collegial team players and avoid necessary conflicts. In an effort to spare other people's feelings, they capitulate in negotiations when it doesn't make sense. They make premature concessions when they should hold their ground. They give feedback that is confusing or vague. This emerges when colleagues avoid transmitting signals to others that might impact their relationships. Instead of speaking honestly and confronting problems head-on, they retreat from the prospect of disagreement. When people avoid conflict, they lose opportunities for the insights and breakthroughs that often emerge from disagreement.

THE COMMUNICATION TRAP

"The information revolution may have increased the amount and speed of communication, but it hasn't improved the quality of communication and people's ability to understand each other, leading to the Communication Trap. The vast amount of data and information leaders get and ask for can make for ineffective discussions and misguided decisions. While technology offers more opportunity to connect with diverse people to attain novel ideas, it does not replace actual face time to ask, listen and converse. There is so much information coming at us that we don't know what to do with it. The situation is chaotic. Meeting after meeting hearing the same information over and over, without new ideas.

THE MACRO-MANAGEMENT TRAP

"We've all heard of micromanagers who hover over their employees and control their every move. Macro-management is micromanagement's lesser-known, but extremely costly, opposite. Macro-management can lead us to pay insufficient attention to details, leaving inadequate structure for people to operate within. They create teams, committees, and task forces to solve problems, expecting them to spontaneously create value and synergy, without establishing the conditions to make that happen or stepping in when there are challenges."[15]

A 2015 Fast Company article talked about a simple daily exercise construct created by Chris Holmberg that can free leaders from traps. The construct was taken from something called 'integral theory' that encourages looking at the world through the lenses of the "It", the "We", and the "I". Holmberg says: "The 'It' refers to your tasks, the external stuff of your role at work: your goals, achievements against those goals, the stuff you are getting done. The 'We' is about your relationships, the quality of your interactions, and the 'I' is about the attitudes and energy you personally bring to the table every day. These moments of reflection are your chance to review and gradually shift your mental models to leading, not just executing and managing."[16]

Revisit Your Day Questions

The It: "Did you execute your work—the emails you wanted to write, the strategy document you owed your boss—the stuff you had on your list at the start of the day? Did you do the things that were important and not just urgent?"

The We: "Did you add value to the lives of the people you interacted with? Did they walk away with more knowledge, energy, goodwill, help, a better understanding? It's not asking whether you made people happy, that's not always the goal. You want to make sure you communicated clearly in a way that added value for them and met goals for you.

The I: "How did you manage your own energy and mood? Self-care measures like working out, eating well, and sleeping enough are just as important as anything you do in the office. The "I" is the foundation of leadership. You can't help others if you deplete yourself."[16]

After you've reflected on the day gone by (it's good to run this practice in the evening shortly before bed), you can use the same three lenses to set your intentions for tomorrow. Here's a template.

Intentions For Tomorrow Questions

The It: "Establish the tasks you intend to accomplish during the day and realistically acknowledge the ones that you won't be able to finish. Do you have meetings during the day? If so, do you know what they're each for? Do you know what you're trying to accomplish during them? Do you have your agenda for reaching those goals?

The We: "Do you anticipate having challenging interactions? For example, do you have any meetings with a colleague who you know is frustrated with you or the company? Think about how you want to show up to that conversation. Consider what he or she might say that will trigger you to react badly. Mentally rehearse how you'd like to respond instead. Write it down and internalize it. Make that your intention.

The I: "What biases do you bring with you? How can you see through them? How can you set yourself up to make good choices throughout the day (i.e. keeping energy high, your body fuelled, etc.)? What might cause you to step off track? What is the right course of action? Identify it ahead of time." [16]

Watch out for arrogance and deference in all your relationships. Holmberg offers this advice: "Replace arrogance with confidence. And swap deference for humility. These might sound like fine distinctions, but in making them, you're retaining your power while combatting ignorance. Once you trust yourself to think critically about others' opinions and humbly adjust your own when necessary, you've found a healthy path: openness." [16]

The road to poor leadership is paved with good intentions. I meant well is not enough. Be alert to the traps. Connect the traps to your reflections on the impact of: ignoring blind spots, being naive about relationships, pursuing simplistic answers, declaring victory to soon, failing to adapt, devaluing others, dominating and abdicating.

To which traps are you and your team most susceptible? Think of which traps are most prominent in your organization. Pick one or two areas you can improve on in coming months.

For each trap you anticipate facing, ask two things. First, what is the result I want? (Define winning.) This will help you choose your strategy. Second, how do I want to show up? (Define personal success.) This will help you keep the discipline of operating within your values.

HUMAN HARD DRIVES
AND BLIND SPOTS

We are a system (an individual) living and working within a human system (your organization). Within yourself as a system, your interest, your fears, your various loyalties all interact and affect your behaviours and decisions. Our "human hard drives" have been shaped, and continue to be shaped, by our perspectives, perceptions, reactions, and expectations. As our human hard drive swells with personal insights and understandings, we develop various coping mechanisms, biases, and habits to protect them (firewalls, anti-virus 'software' and security 'programs'). Our human hard drive continuously validates and defines what we experience by establishing and then attaching, meaning (including truth and untruth) to the experience.

Ron Short, in *Learning in Relationship,* shares important insights into how we act and interact with others. "We share a basic dilemma and potential barrier with everybody else. We live a rich life inside our own head. We continually react, interpret, infer and provide meaning to our own experiences. We create, author, edit, produce, direct and act in our own internal drama. Others do not know or understand what goes on inside of us unless we tell them, but people often assume they do know what we are thinking or wanting—so they never ask. Everyone we work with have rich lives inside their heads too. They also react, interpret, infer, and provide meaning to what happens to them. We are unable to decipher what percolates within them unless they share, but we often assume we know and fail to inquire." [17]

Everything flows from these simple facts. This quote from William James sums it up: "Whenever two people meet, there are really six people present. There is each person as they see themselves, each person as the other person sees them, and each person as they really are."[18]

Blind Spots

For decades, we have attempted to improve how we lead and organize ourselves in business and the public sector, the civil sector, protective services, health sector, education, etc. Progress has been made due to the highly educated population from which we recruit, and the advanced approaches to training development within organizations. We have a very talented and capable workforce. Yet most of us are too familiar with the notion that 'the left hand did not know what the right hand was doing.' Despite the tremendous aptitude within our organizations, communication remains a key challenge. We have accumulated a large repertoire of organizational innovations and a rich array of approaches to organizational change. Yet there is growing concern about the remarkable lack of lasting success. The challenges are replicated across all sectors, and for the matter, across borders.

Practical concepts, frameworks, and tools to improve leadership and organizational cultures have been developing over the past twenty-five years. Edgar Schein, in *Organizational Culture and Leadership,* was the first to elaborate on the significance of (and articulate principles of) working with organizational culture. Other thought leaders, like Kim Cameron in *Diagnosing Organizational Culture* and Robert Quinn in *Discovering the Leader Within,* developed a competing-values framework and a related instrument for engaging members of organizations in discussions about organizational culture. Brian Hall and Richard Barrett, in *New Leadership Paradigm,* articulated theoretically based developmental frameworks, and they generated instruments to 'measure' values and culture to align corporate and member values as part of delivering organizational change that radically reduced wasted resources and energy, significantly improved employee satisfaction, and enormously improved the financial picture. These practical approaches, based in developmental-leadership mindset shifts, are especially helpful to our discussion here because they chart the contrast between the leadership we have and the leadership we need for sustainable change to meet the challenges of dynamic and unpredictable context.

This Albert Einstein quote on unpredictable context is familiar to most people: "The significant problems we face today cannot be solved at the same level of thinking we were at when we created them."[19]That means stepping away from traditional leadership models and making way for new practices. It isn't a new-age theory; it's a fact of life as you embrace the next generation of leaders.

Taylor and MacLeod, in an essay called "Bridging the Leadership Gap," offered the following observations about the next generation of leaders: "For the most part, leaders have been appointed because they are capable of leading the organizations we have. These are largely bureaucratic hierarchies, whether in the public or private sectors. That 20th century organizational model is firmly rooted in a mechanistic worldview in which the leader, as 'engineer,' is the source of all significant knowledge about the organization's direction, operation, and what employees should be doing to achieve success. 20th century leadership is focused on ensuring organizational structures, processes, and personnel optimization to produce its product. Attention is directed primarily to organizational strategy, policies and incentives that optimize employee output, maintain administrative responsibility/control structures, and provide problem-solving capacity. While enlightened bureaucratic leaders have softened this with extensive consultation, the discourse is focused on the 'what' and 'how' with decision-making authority delegated downwards from 'the top'. This approach to leadership and organization began 100 years ago and is out of synch with today's highly educated and networked employees, instantaneous communication capacity, and a global context of accelerating change that demands continuous adaptation."[20]

Otto Scharmer, in his book *Learning from the Future as it Emerges,* invites us to see the world in new ways. He speaks about the leader's blind spot: a disconnect from the source from which they lead. "We know a great deal about what leaders do and how they do it. But we know little about the inner place, the source from which they operate."[21]

It is this fundamental discovery of the blind spot that allows the leader to see what cannot be seen with the eyes, hear what is not said with words, feel what is felt only from the soul, and known from a shared consciousness. Richard Barrett, in *New Leadership Paradigm*, talks about the higher levels of leadership consciousness, where the focus is on cultural cohesion and alignment, building mutually beneficial alliances and partnerships, long-term sustainability, and social respect. Jim Collins, in *Good to Great*, calls it 'level 5 leadership,' which he says, "builds enduring greatness through a paradoxical combination of personal humility and professional will."[22] They change their ego needs away from themselves and into the larger goal of building a great company. It is not that level-5 leaders have no ego or self-interest. Indeed, they are incredibility ambitious, but their ambition is first and foremost for the company, not themselves. Collins calls this "ambition not for themselves but for their companies,"[22] and Barrett highlights "focus on the common good."[23] Isn't that what leading is all about? Moving people, a culture, and an organization forward to something better and greater for all? Leading towards an emerging future? It requires leaders who embody integrity, authenticity, courage, compassion, empathy, humility, and passion. It also requires these leaders to embody fluidity, foresight, and inclusiveness.

We each innately hold certain skills, abilities, and capacities. Not everyone holds the inner state of true leadership. Followers today are looking to leaders who they believe have the capacity to create the space and energy for an emerging possibility. Leaders today must express and personify, or embody, a way of being that exemplifies that which they are impassioned to transform. They connect with an inner source that contains insight to self and the whole. In today's environment, followers are less willing to give their power away to someone else and more likely to engage in a mutually respectful relationship with someone who envelops a vision of wholeness and has an ability to draw out the gifts of those who align with them to achieve extraordinary results.

Daniel Goleman is his book, *Primal Leadership: Unleashing the Power of Emotional Intelligence*, suggests "actions of the leader account for up to 70 percent of employees' perception of the climate of their organization. Emotional intelligence is a key element of self-awareness and the ability to self regulate. The leader personifies this capacity. This is the embodiment of self-integration."[24]

My experiences with emotional intelligence allowed me to see the power of harnessing and leveraging four overlapping points of observation. The four leverage points will be discussed in more detail in the Chapters that follow:

DEALING WITH PATTERNS

The role of the leader is to preconceive specific strategies and recognize the emergence of patterns, intervening when appropriate.

SEEING INTO THE FUTURE

Once people begin to see systemic patterns and understand the forces driving a system, they start to see where the system is headed if nothing is changed. "Seeing into the future" is not a prediction in the statistical sense; it is simply seeing how the system is functioning and where it is headed. Today, the world lacks foresight. The inability or unwillingness to see where we are headed is a massive failure.

TEAM LEARNING

There is enormous need for mastering team learning in organizations. Management teams, product-development teams, and cross-functional teams need to evolve. Teams are micro-manifestations of the collective action desired for the whole. In complexity science, they are fractals of the larger system.

POWERFUL RELATIONSHIPS, NOT POWERFUL INDIVIDUALS

Power is energy, and it needs to flow through organizations. Power cannot be bound or designated to certain functions or levels. What gives power its charge, positive or negative, is the nature of the relationship. If power is generated by our relationships, we need to attend to the quality of those relationships.

Through relationship building, the leader cultivates and unifies teams. In turn, these teams develop their own relationships with others, and as they create effective group dynamics whenever and wherever they interact, they expand the depth of the evolution throughout the organization. As more individuals embrace the vision through a demonstration of value and the creation of win-win alliances, a feeling of ownership for the evolution permeates the culture. This ripple effect happens when the leader embodies an emotional intelligence.

Leadership is often put in context of a hierarchy, with someone who has the command and control of people, things, and processes. The command-and-control form of leadership may work well when the person in the formal leadership position holds all the knowledge and information that is required to achieve certain ordained results. However, in the panacea of today's technology, knowledge and information is available to anyone who wishes to seek it. There is a new freedom to become more, because we are aware there is more.

Like the organization you are trying to lead, you are a complex individual with competing values and interests, preferences, hopes and goals, and accompanying fears. Like everyone else, you have your own default settings: habits of interpreting and responding to people and events around you.

The greatest challenge may be surrendering to self-trust when the ego prefers to take control. It also doesn't mean that a leader is acquiescent; rather it requires knowing when to lead from the front and when to lead from behind. Where are you at on self-trust?

TRUTHS AND UNTRUTHS

My personal career journey of learning provided an opportunity to test and fully appreciate counsel from my greatest mentor: my grandfather. At fifteen, I was about to leave our house for my first formal employment. The job was at a local grocery store, stocking shelves and grocery-bag packing. My grandfather, John MacLeod, called me into his bedroom, and in his typical no-nonsense style, said, "Sit down. I have three pieces of advice."

"LOOK THROUGH AND AROUND THE OBVIOUS"

Over time I began to fully appreciate the wisdom of these words. Leadership is about asking questions, curiosity, testing assumptions, clarity, choice and courage. Leadership is about understanding that organizational systems are made up of many dynamic and emergent human systems. Leadership is about understanding the paradox of simultaneous continuity and change, ambiguity, and complexity. My grandfather often counseled: Understanding happens when you ask questions to test assumptions held, listen to hear and understand first, not to counter first, and have conversations to create new narratives.

"YOUR FREEDOM TO OPERATE MUST BE EARNED"

His message to me was simple—do not tell anyone what you can do; show them what you can do. My experiences with being micro managed and my micro management of others was influenced by actions and results.

"IF YOU TELL THE TRUTH, YOU NEVER HAVE TO REMEMBER"

Unfortunately today we are beginning to see the emergence of a new mantra: If you lie, you never have to remember. Self-reflection is all about looking in the mirror and being truthful about what you see. Can healthy people's relationships be built on untruths?

My grandfather's wisdom was elevated with three overlapping words of wisdom from my labour negotiations mentor Gordon Austin. His words of advice continue to echo in my ears. The first part of negotiations is theatre, and the theatre may last days, weeks, and months. Use the time to ask questions to obtain clarity on what is important, and to find the sweet spot that can lead to a settlement zone. Over time I realized that the theatre Gordon was talking about applies to all human experiences. Special interest and power imbalances are alive and well.

Like my grandfather, his advice on managing self within the theatre was to the point. The most important leadership tool you have in your toolbox is your word; misplaced, you may never get it back. In the heat of a conversation, you can bruise ankles, but never the face. When the going gets tough, and it will, you may want to run. If you don't run, they can't chase you. Leadership is hanging in when the going gets tough. It's about finding a path forward.

We all try to think well of ourselves, but there are lies we can tell ourselves that harm us. Maybe we fear being vulnerable, but we end up insulating ourselves from truth we need, and the leadership cost is high. L. Daskal's leadership blog speaks to ten untruths within ourselves that can either sabotage our success or lead us to greatness.

Even with my grandfather and others whispering in my consciousness, it took me a long time to recognize myself in the following untruths:

> ### Ten Untruths
>
> 1. *"I am in control."* Control is an illusion. Drop the illusion of control and let your leadership lead you.
>
> 2. *"I can do this on my own."* No one does anything alone. Ask yourself who has contributed to your success.
>
> 3. *"I don't have time."* You always have time to do what you believe is important.
>
> 4. *"If I ignore it, it will go away."* You can't change what you refuse to see and confront.
>
> 5. *"I always know best."* Really? Is that the truth? Leadership is about inclusion and learning, not about being right.
>
> 6. *"I'm a good listener."* For leaders, the art of conversation lies in listening.
>
> 7. *"My ego does not get in the way."* Nothing destroys leadership faster than ego.
>
> 8. *"Everybody does it."* You can never be right by doing wrong, and you can never be wrong by doing right.
>
> 9. *"People don't need praise."* What you praise will prosper; what you ignore becomes invisible and ineffective.
>
> 10. *"Emotion is weakness."* The best leaders touch both minds and hearts, and that truth always works."[25]

Do you recognize yourself in any of these untruths? If so, it may be time to have a heart-to-heart talk with yourself.

Dickson and Tholl in *"Bringing Leadership to Life in Health"* suggest leaders need to be self-aware to combat self-delusion. "To combat self-delusion and become more self-aware, each of us as leaders need to first acknowledge our potential for self-delusion and become conscious of our world views, assumptions, and mental models, then rigorously challenge them to root out delusional notions."[14]

Modern leadership is a mind shift from a 20th-century conventional understanding of leadership. The leader understands how organizations are dynamic, living entities that are constantly evolving in the context of an uncertain, unpredictable environment. "Unfortunately, many organizations and leaders continue to demonstrate their industrial-era cultural heritage. In this tradition, the metaphor of a 'well-oiled machine' provides the most trusted and valued model of social organization and has served the needs of a control-based leadership style. However, the information age allows us to constantly create formal and informal shared contexts for senior executives and employees to construct new meaning through their interactions. We must move beyond the old paradigm where leadership resides in a person or role and embrace leadership as a collective responsibility spread across a network of people." [20]

The embodiment of leader, from the micro to the macro, is a journey of embracing being the novice and releasing being the expert. A central component of humanizing leadership is a commitment of leadership towards the greater good of the organization as a whole, its people, and those whom it serves, rather than leader self-aggrandizement. Perhaps the most profound evidence that you have made an impact is when others have been empowered to be the change.

For years, at collective bargaining tables, I repeatedly heard examples about front-line-worker's working conditions and disconnects between middle-managers and the top-executive suite. The union's remedy to the problems identified was a simple quick fix: contractual-process language in the form of new and revised collective-agreement provisions covering a variety of topics, from contracting out, work jurisdiction, scheduling, work assignment, to working conditions. Management's goal was to retard the retreat of management rights.

Can you guess what was missing in the conversation?

ORGANIZATIONAL SPACE CONDITIONS

Imagine an organization as a multi-story building, big and very layered. Leaders have often been far more concerned with the dramas taking place on the upper floors of the building than the relationship breakdowns of people on the floors below. Often, they allowed structure to abrogate relationships.

TOP SPACE CONDITIONS

Have you seen the top level of an organization, which is formally responsible for the whole, dissolve the whole into disintegrated turf domains? Have you seen middle-management sensing, adopting, and mirroring the behaviour of top-level culture, resulting in the erosion of horizontal connections and the mirroring of isolationist behaviours?

As the top and middle level become absorbed in their own aspirations, have you witnessed workers feeling like cogs in a bureaucratic machine, chafing under the remoteness and perceived dysfunction of their bosses? Oshry, in *Seeing Systems,* talks about transforming organizational-system blindness into organizational-system sight to enable people to work together in productive relationships. He suggests "the conditions of the top space in organizations are: responsibility, complexity, and crisis management. The 'blind reflex' to this condition is to suck up responsibility and to feel burdened and overwhelmed. To cope with this feeling, people in the top space differentiate; they retreat to their silos and protect their turf."[26]

Boundary and turf issues often become the norm. Peers begin to protect their domains and resist joint problem solving. When this dividing pattern becomes the organizational norm, it signals to those in the organization to focus narrowly on their individual areas, losing sight of the system as a whole. If we rebuild connections and emphasize common goals, we can stop polarization and isolation from becoming the standard operating style.

MIDDLE SPACE CONDITIONS

"The condition of the middle space is diffusion, the 'torn middles.' Middle-managers are constantly being pulled in numerous directions by the many needs of their subordinates and bosses, as well as by the needs of their customers. The 'blind reflex' to this condition is to disperse—the middle moves towards the individuals that are pulling them. They feel alienated from one another. They are isolated, lonely and fearful of being blamed."[26]

Let's have a closer look at middle-management space, a crucial layer of our organizations. The following analysis and scenario is based on my middle-manager experience in a large organization. The organization was going through a series of restructures and reorganizations resulting in additional and ever-changing workload for management. I was committed to the organization, put in many extra hours, and was very aware of the stress levels within all levels of the organization. With fewer managers, I was given greater responsibility. The number of employees that I managed tripled and spread over a 24/7 clock. Communication linkages were not what they used to be; little time was available for strategic planning, fire-fighting was the norm, and the majority of my time was spent in meetings. Some staff felt guilty bringing new operational issues forward; they saw how busy I was, and they did not want to add an additional burden.

I reported directly to a vice president whose workload was also steadily growing. I wondered whether my boss understood the current state of organizational stability. I also noticed that my boss was becoming more and more preoccupied with senior-management issues, and I felt more and more disconnected. I began to speculate on whether my boss would survive. I missed the mentoring relationship that previously existed. I started to feel fatigued and began questioning my personal effectiveness. At home, I had little to give and was beginning to feel overwhelmed by family tasks.

Capacity is what makes people resourceful, and this human resourcefulness is what organizations count on. Woodward and Wilder talk about three types of capacity: capacity for knowledge and learning, capacity for creating successful relationships, and capacity for enjoyment. Together, these combine to form a resourceful human being. Over development of one of these capacities and neglect of the other two results in reduced capacity, which equates to reduced performance and inability to make change happen.

A critical question to be asked is whether we can identify when capacity erosion is occurring. My middle- management experience provides an illustration and an answer to this question. Previously, I experienced a high degree of work satisfaction and personal growth. I was feeling effective and was considered valuable to the organization. While work was stressful, I received all the necessary information and feedback. However, as the organization underwent constant change, I had lost a sense of connection and satisfaction. I showed signs of capacity erosion. This story is not hypothetical. I was there. How about you?

Middle-managers bridge the ideals and scope of vision from top management with the chaotic reality of the front line. Middle-management is a vehicle for the development of senior managers. Middle-management is an opportunity for individuals to acquire knowledge, become seasoned, test themselves, develop and practice rational and management skills, and gain the required wisdom to lead. We are all too familiar with the words "flatten," "downsize," and "streamline." What if we look inside? What would we find? Is the heart muscle atrophied? Are the electrolytes out of balance? Organizations require strong leadership that will support middle-managers to spread the load. Sufficient downtime is essential, for reflection contributes to collective intelligence. Organizations need the creative process and the collective energy that emanates from people who are given the time and inclination to confront, challenge, play, and listen to one another.

BOTTOM SPACE CONDITIONS

"In the "bottom space" in hierarchical organizations, the condition is one of vulnerability. The behaviour in the bottom space is to coalesce and to "blame up." From the ground perspective, the people "up there" in the c-suite, "up there" in government, the people "up there" in management, and "up there" in governance have had a lot to do with their existing quality of work life."[26] The front lines are often caught between competing organizational imperatives that bring them into conflict with their peers. They feel unified as victims and divided by the absence of common direction and purpose. Imagine the benefits everyone can gain by building bridges between people, with friction and negative energy replaced with enthusiasm, hope, and confidence.

This message to me from a front-line worker speaks volumes to the points made above. It seems to me that reflection, time to reflect, and recognition of the importance of doing so, are often in short supply within organizations. Other things in short supply include ongoing personal relationships among staff (undermined by high turnover), information (lack of communication tools), and the ability to say what one really thinks (without jeopardizing employment). Clichéd words like "system," "transformation," "leadership," "innovation," and "sustainability" are used so frequently, and in so many different contexts, that they have become meaningless.

So, here is a recap of important elements that create a feeling of vulnerability in the "bottom space" of hierarchal organizations: insufficient information, lack of long-standing collegial relationships, wariness of speaking openly, an overuse of clichés, self-serving experts from the outside who have never worked in the environment, and no time to really think about what is happening.

In a future-focused learning organization, front-line workers take responsibility for their own condition and the condition of the organization. They pull together as a positive force for change and improvement. They are empowered to control and coordinate their work.

The truth is that all the answers can be found in the hearts and minds of people. Every individual has the capacity to contribute to organizational growth. Individuals carry the seeds of success: skills, talents, potentialities, and enthusiasm. Unfortunately, for many those same seeds contain too many intellectual emotional, and systemic barriers. Liberating the "bottoms" and integrating the "middles" is how learning organizations succeed.

Two Organizational Portraits

1. *People Are Torn* between multiple objectives and dazed by the introduction of one priority after another. People tend to pay lip service to initiatives but develop many ways to beat the system. People become masters at giving a presentation of change without actually changing.

2. *People Are Self-Directed and Multi-Skilled.* Relationships between the members and teams consist of mutual interdependence. Leaders and followers are able to easily switch roles. Existing groups are open and unrestrictive. People can enter and leave with minimum hassle. Silos are open and undefended. Values influence the dynamics at every level. An acceptance and responsibility for personal self-management and formal organizational management exists throughout. Actions take place within the context of 'immediate return' economies with short feedback loops between action and result that maximize learning and performance improvement.

What portrait best captures your organization or the department you have responsibility for? What's your contribution to the portrait? What needs to change?

How healthy is your middle-management and front line organizational space? What behaviour is the top mirroring to the other spaces?

ORGANIZATIONAL WHITE SPACE

The purpose of an automobile is to take you from one place to another. No single part of an automobile can get you there. A well functioning automobile is not the sum of its parts. It is the alignment, fluidity, and interconnectivity of the moving parts that takes you to another place.

Organizations are no different. Yes leaders of today's corporations may have built the engine and chassis, filled the tank with high octane fuel and turned the key, but in many cases, they are still learning how to accelerate, shift gears, brake and navigate in a global market place, and within the spaces of the complex human organizational systems they built.

Organizations work by connections. These include the prescribed connections of the hierarchy, formal business processes, assigned teams and the structures put in place by management. Other organizational structures are emergent, and they are neither designed, nor engineered. These include advice, expertise, support, mentoring and leadership relationships that emerge during the course of business. Employees form these connections to get their job done; especially when their formal workflow is either broken, blocked, or behind schedule.

We portray prescribed and emergent organizational spaces on organizational charts that are finely drafted confines. As Marshal McLuhan taught us, we need to pull ourselves out of our everyday use of a particular information system, like an organizational map, and stand back to analyze what the very existence of the information tells us about ourselves. As McLuhan succinctly put it, "the medium is the message." [27]

The 'organizational chart map' is essentially an aggregate of isolated power blocks with a steep hierarchy command center. Organizational static box images imply rigid turf boundaries, drawn with black boxes and lines on blank white paper, whereas high-performing organizations draw out the dynamic and fluid white space between all the lines and organizational boxes. There's a lot of whitespace. That's the informal organization - relationships and loyalties that exist outside formal reporting structures, resources that seem to come from nowhere, and projects that proceed outside the normal management control processes. All kinds of things happen in whitespace, from critical idea exchange around the coffee machine to the creation of entire new business lines.

White space is the organizational space in which people operate and interact. It is also an organizational space where there is a huge amount of human pain and wasted resources because of human interactions that produce misattribution and misunderstood and misinterpreted information. It is often what happens in the white space on the organization chart that is key to effective learning organizations.

White space is a process-management concept described by Rummler and Brache in *Improving Performance: How to Manage White Space* as the area between the boxes in an organizational chart where no one is usually in charge. It is where important handoffs between functions happen, and where an organization has the greatest potential for improvement. It is a space where things often "fall between the cracks" or "disappear into black holes."

Maletz and Nohria, in *Managing White Space*, describe it as an area within a company where the existing corporate culture does not apply. Where rules are vague, authority is fuzzy, budgets are nonexistent, and strategy is unclear. The authors offer the following insights: "Whitespace exists in all companies, and enterprising people are everywhere testing the waters with unofficial efforts to boost the bottom line. The managers who operate in these uncharted seas are often the ones most successful at driving innovation, incubating new businesses, and finding new markets. The task for senior managers is to avoid letting whitespace efforts just happen. Instead, they should actively support and monitor these activities, even as they keep them separate from the organization's formal work. If companies leave this valuable territory to the scattershot whims and talents of individual managers, they are likely to miss out on many of the opportunities that come from exploring the next frontier."[28]

A. Hartung, in *Pursuing White Space Opportunity,* describes white space as a place that provides a location for new thinking, testing and learning. He cites examples of companies that used the white space to evolve new formulae for business success that is free of existing defend and extend culture. Powerful dimensions of organizational life are invisible. A shift of attention towards white space needs to occur in order to illuminate critical qualities that shape organizational life, the experience of the workplace, and the capacity to deliver results. We must become aware of the connection between our experience of others and the systemic conditions we are in, and we need to develop and maintain partnerships and strengthen our relationships. In other words, instead of fixing one another, we need to work together to master the influencing conditions.

Paying attention to and understanding organizational space relationships has the power to prevent organizations from falling into holes and finding new paths forward. Since people are the vectors of those relationships, understanding and nurturing their intrinsic motivation is key. Through discourse and the application of honest conversation, we can keep the fire burning. If this fire is ignited in enough people, organizations can outgrow any and all of the space-condition challenges they face.

Reflect on the paradoxes contained within the following organizational portraits. Loyalty and exemplary performance is no longer grounds for an ascent up the corporate ladder. A flattening of the hierarchical structures, along with the surge of baby-boomers entangled within the systems core, makes the traditional path towards the top improbable. The loss of critical organizational memory is now balanced with book intellectual learning and consultants on contract. Full-time employment eroded by part-time and casual employment. Technology is advancing at an unprecedented pace and some are questioning people and organizational capacity to keep up. Experience and intuitive prowess is not exclusively acquired through simulation or theoretic applications. Vital skills are no longer learned and handed down in an apprentice, coaching, mentoring like manner. Teamwork is better that the sum of individual effort, while at the same time the group is vulnerable to the weakest member of the team. Today's business leaders are often running a full-time sprint just to keep up with the day-to-day demands of business.

Unfortunately many organizations and leaders are not equipped to deal with this new reality. Leaders built human organizational systems based on their assumption of a linear world; so they build neat looking organizational boxes of departments, hierarchies and reporting lines. The portraits above demands agility, adaptability, innovation for all, but many organizations still reward status and conformity.

The portraits of paradox beg an important question, how does an organization deliver quality services, products, and/or experiences when its most valuable asset is under threat? If an employee feels dissatisfied, unchallenged, and unable to contribute in his or her professional life, his or her overall performance will be substandard. Our policies and mandates alone do not alter the way people within our organizations interact, communicate, and function. Organizations must express gratitude for the essential intellectual, emotional, and physical contributions of the workforce. Outcomes and output are dictated by the outlook and sensibilities of the employees. Studies clearly demonstrate how productivity drops significantly when people feel detached. On the flip side, hope and confidence can grow and spread like wildfire, and when people feel honoured and valued, their energy and enthusiasm become infectious.

Our leadership behaviour is often honed in a manner that allows for operational and political survival; playing the game of passive aggression, protecting the silo at all costs, while failing to recognize the connectivity (and leverage opportunities) between independence and system interdependence. Survival mode often ushers us towards quick fixes, unsustainable change, and unintended consequences for all the challenges and opportunities before us.

Everything leaders engage in has an element of confrontation: a clash of priorities, a struggle for the status quo, and a battle of beliefs. Every day, leaders experience the political and organizational "urgencies" of a top space, and the conflict between planning and the daily demands of the position. Life is full of paradoxes and uncertainties. As we will later discus in more detail, there are paradoxes at the heart of everything, and they cannot be solved. Acceptance is the only way to tackle paradox—to learn from, cope with, and manage the contradictions and discontinuities they impart, forging a reconciliation of opposites. Paradoxes add to the complexities of leadership.

Bottom line, paradox is inevitable, endemic, and perpetual; the more turbulent the times, and the more complex the world, the more paradoxes there are. We can and should reduce the starkness of some of the contradictions, minimize the inconsistencies, and understand the puzzles in the paradoxes, but we cannot make them disappear, solve them completely, or escape from them. To be a leader of change in this complex environment, a leader combines and integrates ideas, even when they appear contradictory of one another. Leaders find the "sweet spot" between the fundamentally paradoxical notions.

How are you developing the personality, the conceptual ability, the artistic temperament, and the practice of successful juxtaposition of opposites to find the sweet spot?

To humanize leadership we will have to overcome the closed and often fragmented boxes on the organizational chart and embrace the space between the boxes, imbuing it with deeper meaning and purpose.

As a leader, how are you leveraging the informal organizational spaces?

EVERYONE WANTS TO CHANGE
AND NO ONE WANTS TO CHANGE

With the support of Longwoods Publishing a collection of twenty-one open letters from acknowledged healthcare leaders was published between 2016 and 2017. My invitation to the authors included the following passage; a goal of the open letters is to create new leadership and change conversations between governance and senior-management, and middle-management, and care providers. While the invitation went out to healthcare leaders the opinions shared in the open letters apply to both public and private sector organizations. For the purposes of this book I chose to highlight opinions from two open letters.

On the topic of personal change; author and educator Dr. Graham Dickson's, open letter titled *"Leadership Inaction Or Leadership In Action – The Change Dilemma"*, summed it up nicely: "The old adage that everyone wants change but no one wants to change is prevalent. Corporate boards, governments, and non-profits call for transformation, yet many are unwilling to transform their own behaviour. Everyone wants collective efforts, but no one want to partner with each other because they are afraid of losing control of the agenda. Everyone wants a well-honed, integrated system, but they also want to retain independence and autonomy from that system. We all want collaboration, shared visions, and collective action to achieve change, but when pressed to deliver, we often revert to demands of ego, turf, and combativeness. It seems that we intellectually "buy" the notion of transformation, but we are not ready to accept the personal demands associated with its success. Instead of leadership in action—championing and orchestrating change—we have leadership inaction, with a lot of talk and little to no action."[29]

Arlinda Ruco's, open letter titled *"What I Learned From My Personal Board Of Directors"* talks about three take-a-ways for any emerging leader to adopt in order to propel their professional and personal development forward. The idea of a 'personal board of directors' comes from the work of Jim Collins who suggests leaders should define an informal group of people who serve as a mechanism to leverage wisdom, experience and advice that can help navigate difficult or ethical dilemmas. From being in the presence of her personal board of directors, Arlinda suggests the following:

NEVER UNDER ESTIMATE THE POWER OF COFFEE

"You would be surprised how many people are willing to give up 30 minutes of their time with the promise of a free cup of java (or tea). This was one of the strategies I used to secure the time of those who I did not formally know. Offering to buy someone coffee is a great strategy for building new relationships and getting to know people outside of their work titles. You might be surprised at what you end up learning about people in the process and how valuable these interactions can be to your own development. Every time you sit down with someone new for a cup of coffee, ask them who else they would recommend you meet with. This can continue to build your professional network and is a great way to recruit people for your Board of Directors.

DON'T LEAVE WITHOUT A BOOK RECOMMENDATION

"Although the time and discussions had with each member of my Board were instrumental to my development and growth, I didn't want my learning to stop there. One of the most valuable things I did was to ask these leaders for some of their top book recommendations. I then got my hands on copies of these books and read them one by one. Not all of the books that were recommended resonated with me, but they all made me question, think and reflect on my own core values and beliefs. In addition, the great thing about book recommendations is that you can pay them forward and share them with other leaders who may reach out to you.

NEVER TURN DOWN THE OPPORTUNITY TO GET OUT OF YOUR OFFICE

"One of the best observations I made in my personal Board of Directors was that these leaders rarely turned down the opportunity to get out of their office, in fact they welcomed it. This may have taken them some additional time to coordinate or for travel, but it afforded them a deeper understanding and appreciation for the work of others. In addition, it was experiences like these that continued to fuel their own creativity and inspired their out of the box thinking."[30]

A leader's behaviour must adapt based on situational moderators. The core assumption is that a leader must assess relationships between follower(s) and task(s) to be accomplished while also recognizing the intervening variables. These variables pertain to the things outside of the leader's control that could influence the outcome. Leadership needs to be concerned with both human relationships and the accomplishment of tasks. The effectiveness of a leader is highly dependent upon their ability to modify their approach due to the differing circumstances or context of each situation. They must be versatile, flexible, and competent at determining the appropriate style to implement and be competent in using it. The overall effectiveness of a leader is contingent upon how appropriate and effective their chosen leadership style tackles any given work situation.

Sustainable transformation is based on an empowering environment where a commitment to, and alignment of, followers to corporate goals and objectives is established. Leaders in this environment influence followers' consciousness by appealing to higher ideals and moral values. The levels of trust, respect, and loyalty are measured by what leaders extend to followers. About 2,500 years ago, Chinese philosopher Lao Tzu eloquently expressed the idea of individuals who catalyze collective leadership: "The wicked leader is he whom the people despise. The good leader is he whom the people revere. The great leader is he of whom the people say, "We did it ourselves."[31]

The Oxford Dictionaries defines "self-awareness" as the *"conscious knowledge of one's own character and feelings."* It's built on an honest assessment and reflection on one's personality, character, strengths, weaknesses, beliefs, values, motives, and desires. Self-aware leaders become comfortable looking in the mirror—accustomed to seeing ourselves for who we are. The mirror acts as a catalyst to help identify what changes you need to make. In the same way, self-awareness is a catalyst for personal development, change, and growth. Self-awareness is the foundation of all personal and leadership development.

Peter Drucker, in *"Managing Knowledge Means Managing Oneself,"* offers a view that successful leaders exploit their strengths and manage their weaknesses. While you and I may be good at many things, we are only really great at a few things. Self-aware leaders know the few things they are great at and are constantly working on improving on these few key strengths. They have a firm grasp of their capabilities and are less likely to set themselves up to fail by, for example, over-stretching on assignments. They know, too, when to ask for help. And the risks they take on the job are calculated; they won't ask for a challenge they know they can't handle alone. They play to their strengths.

With self-reflection and honesty, one can recognize how the image we attempt to portray does not necessarily mirror the reality in which we find ourselves. Like a photographer, leaders must make a number of choices to capture or address the subject at hand. They must choose what to focus on, how to frame it, what elements get highlighted, and the overall composition. Capturing the environment at different moments and angles, each snapshot is its own slice of reality. In order to capture the perfect image, they make continual adjustments and take multiple attempts, vowing never to stop until their image mirrors their vision. Leadership is about continuous learning from the images that capture progression; even the images that represent the negative side. Through a dissection of displeasing elements that plague us, we are able to come to new understandings and finally move beyond them. An organizational system is much deeper and more complex than any curated gallery will ever depict. Moments of personal reflection enable us to undertake our key responsibility, which is to create the conditions within to outgrow today's challenges.

Self-awareness helps you to identify thinking, beliefs, and behaviours to improve your leadership. It's self-awareness that helps you address gaps in your leadership. It's self-awareness that triggers your desire for change. It's self-awareness that keeps you growing. It's an interesting paradox: I learn more about myself so I can focus better on others. And by focussing on the development of others, high-performing environments are created in which people feel safe, take on more risk, and grow in the process.

Exercising personal reflection as a guide, leaders can act on a key responsibility, which is to create the systemic conditions that will generate solutions to current challenges within organizations.

Real leadership is not a demand for power or acquiescence to the demand. Leadership is earned. Leaders excel because they continuously ask questions of themselves and others. The leader of a learning organization knows how to frame the right question, the timing of its asking, and how it is asked. The framed question needs to be posed in a manner that creates commitment to a cause and a challenge to other people.

On your leadership journey ask this question continually: How can I create a culture that encourages the expression of intelligence, passion, commitment, and experience by people at all levels of the organization?

Answering this question has far-reaching implications for selection criteria, leadership development, mentoring, and coaching.

MOVING FORWARD

Leadership is about inspiring others to do their best, and to enable decision-making at every level of the organization. It is about recognizing and valuing the contributions of others and demonstrating astute confidence and trust in the ability of individuals and teams to coordinate and control their own work.

Leaders model for others how a team can operationalize a strategic direction with the right balance of management/leadership, which will enable the whole organization to accelerate its transformation. Leaders take action and nurture the "people matter" and "relationships make the difference" seeds that allow for a connected human system.

W. Brian Arthur, in *Sense Making in the New Economy*, wrote the following: "To change the quality of an organizational field, the fire in your belly combined with intention is not the most powerful force, it is the only force."[32]

Intention and personal character are linked. Unfortunately this linkage gets played out daily, leading to distrust for leaders. This crisis of confidence in leadership is present not only in business, but also in government, and public administration, entertainment, sports and religious organizations. In all of this, the role of character resurfaces time and time again as a contributing culprit.

I hope you do not gloss over "intentions and character" as you move forward on your personal leadership path. Based on research involving over three hundred leaders from different sectors and countries, Crossman, Seijts, and Ganz developed a model of eleven leadership virtues for character building.

Let's Imagine the Following Leadership Virtues:

1. *"Passion:* an essential fire in the belly to make things happen. Without passion, leaders cannot fully drive energy, ignite others, raise influence, or provide potential. The inherent intensity and will to get things done creates results.

2. *Humility*: essential to learning and becoming a better leader. Without humility, a lack of open-mindedness will prevent the leader from soliciting or considering the views of others. They can't learn from others or reflect critically on their failures to become better leaders as a result of those reflections. They become caricatures of themselves, resulting in isolation.

3. *Integrity:* essential to building trust and encouraging others to collaborate. Without integrity, leaders cannot build solid relationships with followers, with their organizational superiors, with allies, or with partners. Every promise has to be guaranteed, and the resulting mistrust slows down decisions and actions.

4. *Collaboration:* enables teamwork. Without collaboration, leaders will fail to achieve worthwhile goals that require more than individual effort and skills. They don't use the diversity of others' knowledge, experience, perceptions, judgments, and skills to make better decisions and to execute them better.

5. *Justice:* yields decisions that are accepted as legitimate and reasonable by others. Without a sense of justice, leaders are unable to understand the issues of social inequality and the challenges associated with fairness. Such leaders act in unfair ways and reap negative consequences in the form of poor employee relations or reactions by customers, governments, and regulators. People will find ways to undermine the leader.

6. *Courage*: helps leaders make difficult decisions and challenge the decisions or actions of others. Without courage, leaders will not stand up to poor decisions made by others and will lack the perseverance and tenacity required to work through difficult issues. They will also back down in the face of adversity and choose the easy route.

7. *Temperance*: ensures that leaders take reasonable risks. Without temperance, leaders take un-calculated risks, rush to judgment, fail to gather relevant facts, have poor sense of proportion, and make frequent and damaging changes or even reverse important decisions.

8. *Accountability:* ensures that leaders own and commit to the decisions they make and encourages the same in others. Without accountability, leaders don't commit to, or own, the decisions they make, and cannot get others to do so. They blame others for poor outcomes, creating a culture of fear and disengagement. Disastrous consequences unfold when people stop caring.

9. *Humanity:* builds empathy and understanding of others. Without humanity, leaders are unable to relate to others, see situations from their followers' perspectives, or take into account the impact of their decisions on others. Without humanity, leaders will not act in socially responsible ways and will alienate people.

10. *Transcendence*: equips the leader with a sense of optimism and purpose. Without transcendence, leaders' goals become narrow and they fail to elevate discussions to higher-order goals. They don't see the bigger picture and their decisions may reflect opportunism only. They don't think outside the box or encourage others to do so.

11. *Judgment:* allows leaders to balance and integrate these virtues in ways that serve the needs of multiple stakeholders in and outside their organizations. Without judgment, leaders make flawed decisions, especially when they must act quickly in ambiguous situations, namely when faced with the many paradoxes that confront all leaders from time to time." [33]

REFLECTIONS AND CONSIDERATIONS

As leaders, the characteristics we emanate are infectious. Are you aware of the behaviours, language, and demeanour you exhibit? Do these elements mirror your values and ethics?

It is difficult to maintain a high level of enthusiasm over an extended period of time. It is important to understand what invigorates you and your team, so that it can be drawn from when enthusiasm needs to be revived. Are you in touch with what invigorates you and your team?

We all have certain skill sets at which we excel, but we are not exceptional across the entire skill-sets gamut. It is essential to build a solid team around you—a team you trust to make decisions and get things done. When you share responsibility, you build a collaborative organizational culture. Are you utilizing the strengths of those around you? Do you hold the reins too tight? Are the right people in place?

We are products of our personal experiences, and we have tendencies that are often subconsciously applied. In regards to leadership styles, how cognizant are you of the styles you apply to the situations you face? Are you able to maintain a harmonious balance between management and leadership?

Transparency, openness, and acceptance are crucial to our personal leadership development and journey. Do you acknowledge that the stories in our heads are self-composed and singular in perspective? Do you accurately and openly share them? Do you inquire about the perspectives and understandings of others? Do you listen intently to the message being shared? Are you occupied with constructing and presenting your counter? Do you revise our story based upon new pieces of information you receive?

It is deemed unprofessional to make mistakes even though it is human to err. Not knowing an answer to a question within your area of expertise is often internalized as an admission of incompetence. How tightly do you hold on to this unrealistic expectation of leadership and yourself? Why are you a leader? Are you ever really prepared? Why should all those wonderfully talented people who work for you pay any attention to what you are doing?

What makes you lead the way you do? Who or what influenced your experience of leadership? How did they shape your values, tendencies, and biases? Has your view of what it means to lead changed over time?

Are you growing as a leader? How do you measure your growth?

From the book *Learning in Relationship*: "Do you agree with this statement? 'You create the impact others have on you' is without doubt the most difficult and most important leadership lesson to learn. Often we create an image of the way something is supposed to look; when the reality does not match our image, we often simply ignore it." [17]

CHAPTER II
ARE HEARTS, SPIRITS AND MINDS IMPORTANT TO YOU?

"Treat employees like they make a difference and they will."
~ J. Goodnight

INTRODUCTION

The overall success of an organization is not established merely by the completion of tasks or the agendas laid forth, but through the motivation and dedication of its people. The level of dedication is founded on, and fluctuated by, feelings of inclusion, recognition, ability to contribute, and the opportunity for growth. When people feel voiceless or insignificant, every other aspect of them tends to mirror that feeling of vulnerability.

In Chapter II, I discuss how a primary task of leadership should be to develop the organization's most critical asset: its dedicated people. I ask, are the five words "people are our greatest asset" the most meaningless words in our organizational vocabulary? A number of statistics on the workplace health begin to set a human paradox. I explore how people issues impact organizational goals and how empathy can be a foundation for people matter conversations. This leads to a discussion about leveraging values, principles and ethics, and the power of honouring diversity. I end with a question; does culture eats strategy for breakfast?

PEOPLE "ARE" OUR GREATEST ASSET

We find the "people are our greatest asset" concept within the frame of value statements that include words such as 'respect,' 'trust,' 'diversity,' and 'openness.' Far too often, this is merely wallpaper within a picture frame with no commitment to alter the organizational mindset.

Are the five words people are our greatest asset the most meaningless words in our organizational vocabulary? Can you provide examples of what your organization does to give all employees the feeling that they are the most important assets? Does your organization pay the same amount of attention to employees as it does to customers? Does the people asset get as much management time discussion as the fiscal assets?

Most organizations follow business protocol and report physical and financial assets on their balance sheets, often neglecting the human component of business all together. The sum of an organization's patents, processes, employees' skills, technologies, information about customers and suppliers, and old-fashioned expertise constitutes the true value of a business or organization. The viability of an organization is contingent on its human, physical, and financial assets, and how these specific components are leveraged. The absolute worth of an organization cannot be understood unless human value is incorporated.

To make the 'people an asset' metaphor reality, we must be inclusive. We must deal with many factors we cannot control. Even in these situations, we must fight the normal tendency to pull inward; we need to maintain open communications and conversation links with people and decision-making processes. We must engage people's faculties of reflection, feedback, and decision-making. We must also achieve sterling performance under conditions of extreme fiscal pressures and increasing service and customer demands. These are not mutually exclusive. Richard Branson, founder of the Virgin business lines, said, "Clients do not come first; employees come first. If you take care of your employees, they will take care of their clients."[1] Do you agree?

Depending on your age, you may remember a circle dance called the "Hokey Pokey," in which everyone stands around in a circle, and at different stages of the dance, you are asked to put different parts of your body into the circle: left hand, right hand, left foot, right foot, left shoulder, right shoulder, head, and finally your whole body. The goal is to get your whole self into the circle and "shake it all about."

When we get mind, body, and spirit in the circle, we are beginning to function holistically. "Our mind is in the circle when we have an intention as to what we want to do. Our body is in the circle when we act with skill to carry out our intention. It encompasses how we go about achieving our intention. When our spirit is in the circle, we can determine if what we are doing is right, and if our motives are aligned with our internal moral compass. When all three are brought to bear, our power increases, our wisdom increases, and our effectiveness as leaders increases.[2]

On the subject of mind, body, and spirit a number of studies paint an alarming picture. A study by Kronos and Future Workplace found that 95 percent of human-resource leaders admit that employee burnout is sabotaging workforce retention, yet there is no obvious solution on the horizon. In this national survey, 614 HR leaders—including Chief Human Resource Officers (CHRO), vice presidents of HR, HR directors, and HR managers from organizations with 100 to 2,500+ employees provided a candid look at how burnout drives turnover, what causes it, and why there is no easy solution despite 87 percent of respondents calling improved retention a high/critical priority.

According to the survey, "nearly half of HR leaders (46 percent) say employee burnout is responsible for up to half (20 to 50 percent, specifically) of their annual workforce turnover. While many organizations take steps to manage employee fatigue, there are far fewer efforts to proactively manage burnout. Not only can employee burnout sap productivity and fuel absenteeism, but as this survey shows, it will undermine engagement and cause an organization's top performers to leave the business altogether. This creates a never-ending cycle of disruption that makes it difficult to build the high-performing workforce needed to compete in today's business environment."[3]

Day in and day out, organizations deliver exceptional service through passionate and skilled workers. Yet, many have a serious health issue. A high rate of occupational injury and absence is resulting in extraordinary productivity and payroll loss due to long-term disability, workplace injury, and sick leave. For example, a Truven Health Analytics report suggests that hospital employees are less healthy than the general workforce and cost more in healthcare spending. They found "hospital employees are more likely to be diagnosed with chronic conditions like asthma, obesity, and depression, and were five (5) percent more likely to be hospitalized. These workers spent nine (9) percent more in healthcare costs than the general public."[4]

PUTTING A PRICE ON NOT CARING ABOUT EMPLOYEES

A recent study by Menon and Thompson asked eighty-three USA executives (70 percent male; 87 percent with more than ten years of work experience, with 45 percent having ten years or more in senior-management roles) to put a price on the amount their companies lost each day due to a range of people issues, from interpersonal conflicts and unproductive weekly staff meetings to hiring the wrong employees and investing in training and development programs that don't work. The study authors expected the study to reveal significant waste. However, they were not ready for the magnitude of the results. "In the course of a day, the executives estimated wasting an average of $7,227.07 per line item per day, for a total of $144,541.30 per day, summing each of the twenty points of waste. That's an astounding $52,757,574 of lost value and potential per year per organization on people problems. These are perceptions rather than scientific measures, but they reveal significant amounts of lost value."[5]

Other studies reveal similar waste. For example, a CCP Incorporated and Thomas Kilman study on workplace conflict found American employers reported spending "2.8 hours per week dealing with conflict, amounting to approximately $359 billion in paid hours, or the equivalent of 385 million working days in the country as a whole. Further, 25 percent of employees said that avoiding conflict led to sickness or absence from work, and nearly 10 percent reported that workplace conflict led to project failure."[6]

A recent study released by the Productivity Commission in Australia found that the "total cost to the economy of bullying and harassment is about $14.8 billion a year."[7] Violence against workers in health-care settings like hospitals, nursing homes, and psychiatric environments is an under-reported, ubiquitous, and persistent problem, says an article published in the New England Journal of Medicine. What's worse, the article says, "It's a problem that's been tolerated and largely ignored. What were once considered to be safe havens are now confronting steadily increasing rates of crime, including violent crimes such as assault, rape and homicide."[8]

Absenteeism is often used as the measure for lost productivity, but it does not reflect the full scope or issues that stem from absenteeism. The term "presenteeism" refers to the loss of productivity and quality of service due to the incapacitated-worker segment—workers impaired physically, cognitively, or emotionally by illness, injury, or workplace culture. Presenteeism is one of the largest threats to productivity, and its impact can rival that of absenteeism. In addition, presenteeism can have far-reaching consequences, affecting coworkers, clients, and vendors alike, which compounds the situation further.

The cost of presenteeism to businesses is approximately ten times higher than absenteeism. "Absent workers cost employers around USD $150 billion per year, but those who came to work and were not fully productive cost USD $1,500 billion per year.[9] According to a report by Global Corporate Challenge, on average, employee absenteeism and presenteeism cost business the equivalent of three months per year in lost productivity. And a recent Harvard study showed that 36 percent of workers suffer from work-related stress that costs U.S. businesses $30 billion a year in lost workdays."[10]

At the heart of most of these apparently intractable issues at work, we usually find a combination of organizational workplace wellness and leadership issues: stress and anxiety, interpersonal conflict, miscommunication, poor decision-making, and more. While these problems can seem tedious or frustrating, the true cost of this class of problems is much more troubling.

Dickson and Tholl, in *"Bringing Leadership to Life in Health,"* put it this way: "A healthy organization is a productive organization characterized by high attendance amongst the people who work there as well as high retention rates and low turn-over. Leaders can create the conditions for a healthy organization. The first thing a good leader can do is signal the importance of being a healthy organization by making it a priority, and gathering data and information related to work-life, quality, both in terms of morale and productivity. Without such data leaders can easily lose touch with the work-life experience of others."[11]

Are you having conversations on the following? Metrics matter, but people matter more; employee engagement and discretionary effort must be led, not managed; a humanizing leader confronts truth within a people-centric philosophy; leadership authenticity begins with personal awareness; the purpose of leadership is to build the next generation of leaders; hope sees the invisible, feels the intangible, and achieves the impossible.

Improving the workplace wellness record would improve the resiliency, adaptability, creativity, satisfaction, morale, and productivity of individual workers. At the organizational level, these changes translate into improved performance, decreased costs, and increased quality. In other words, employee and workplace health is inextricably linked to productivity, high performance, and success. A strategic focus on health and caring for employees would be a unifying thesis in an otherwise divisive and impersonal environment.

How does an organization deliver quality services, products, and/or experiences when its most valuable asset is under threat?

How is your organization, or your department, doing with mind, body, and spirit integration? What needs to change?

SOFT IMPACTS HARD

In his TED Talk on: "*How To Start A Movement*" Derek Sivers analyzed the spontaneous dance of a man at an outdoor concert event. In his talk, Sivers breaks down movement building into three easy steps. Having the guts to stand out and be ridiculed. Embrace early followers as equals. It's the first followers who change others' perceptions of you from a lone nut to a leader. Make sure the movement is public and showcases followers because new members emulate followers not the leader.

Followership will always be in the shadow of leadership. But there are no leaders without followers. Who would not benefit from giving some thought to how they could be a better at creating a follower movement? Such thought may actually hasten your trip to the leadership position you actually want. Simply put, followers are fueled by soft things like organizational culture, teachable moments, effective collaboration, ability to experience change, and learning. Not having followers creates friction with hard things like consumer satisfaction, crisis frequency, retention of staff, cost of performance, cost of service, share holder value, and profit.

The soft stuff is really the hard stuff. The "soft" includes how people think and behave; the organization's human dynamics; the extent to which people experience a safe, supportive environment where there is respect, empathy, and compassion; the degree of internal capacity and skills for strategic and leveraged thinking.

According to a survey by Adeco Staffing USA, 45 percent of executives said a lack of soft skills was the biggest proficiency gap they saw in the U.S. workforce."[12] Research from the Hay Group revealed that organizations who incorporate a range of soft talents into their leadership approach can increase their team's performance by as much as 30 percent. "Without soft skill development organizations can and will encounter more internal conflicts, all of this impacts reputation, brand and profitability."[13]To quote Deloitte's 2015 Report of Global Human Capital Trends, "Softer' areas, such as culture and engagement, leadership, and development, have become urgent priorities."[14] The skills that matter most are the ones we mistakenly called soft. But there is nothing soft about them.

Efficiency alone doesn't make an organization stand out; it also needs to be innovative as well. As we will discuss later, efficiency and innovation each require a different mindset, and what unites both is learning, and that get us into all the soft skills. In an era when companies strive to become more efficient through the use of technology and data, it's easy to dismiss the ability to build relationships and collaborate as nice-to-have rather than need-to-have.

The longer an organization has been in operation, the more likely what occurs in the organizational culture is happening at the level of unconscious norms and basic assumptions built on mental models that are completely out of view. Any challenges to these basic assumptions, which provide individual and shared organizational minds with stability and security, are likely to give rise to anxiety and social-defense mechanisms. As we will discuss in more detail in Chapter III, the social era represents the need to understand how to feed minds. This shift requires an understanding of value created from intangibles such as human relationships, strategic and structural, which is gained by strong minds. A strong mind is not afraid to learn to understand what he/she doesn't know.

Finally, soft variables such as intentions, interpretations, and relationships are considered part of the primary sphere of customer-experience value creation. Leaders will have to learn to pay attention to a different set of variables—the variables referred to as 'soft' relationship skills.

Today is about managing the things that management can count. The future will be about managing the things you can't count or at least you didn't think you could. I hope there will be a sudden awakening of the soft side, realizing the value of stuff like culture, purpose, collaboration, and human relationship capital. I hope all the things that have been traditionally labelled, as the intangibles will become important and visible. It is easy to add, subtract, multiply, divide, and manipulate numbers. It is hard to understand what you do not know, do not control, and do not want to learn from. The awakening of the soft issues represents the need to shift how you manage and lead. Much of this shift is being fuelled by the early outcomes of the Social Era, where power has shifted to the many rather than the few.

Your organization's "soft skill" ability and intelligence will be tested on a regular basis. When there are failures, pressures from the outside, or employee problems, it will be easy to retreat to traditional 'hard skilled' management processes and structures with an illusion of control from the top. The real test for leaders is to discover how much they really trust their employees and honour their voices.

Trust is hard, because it requires a leader to be present, vulnerable, and connected to another human being. You can't practice good coaching, listening, collaboration, or engagement skills alone. You just can't. We practice these skills with others, and in doing so, publicly engage in the process of try-fail-learn-try-succeed-fail-learn over and over again. Burch, in *Learning Stage Model*, talks about conscious incompetence, saying that no matter what new skill we decide to learn there are four learning stages each of us goes through. Being aware of these stages helps us better accept that learning can be a slow and frequently uncomfortable process.

Four Stages of Learning

Stage 1: Unconsciously unskilled. We don't know what we don't know. We are inept and unaware of it.

Stage 2: Consciously unskilled. We know what we don't know. We start to learn at this level when sudden awareness of how poorly we do something shows us how much we need to learn.

Stage 3: Consciously skilled. Trying the skill out, experimenting, practicing. We now know how to do the skill the right way but need to think and work hard to do it.

Stage 4: Unconsciously skilled. If we continue to practice and apply the new skills, eventually we arrive at a stage where they become easier, and given time, even natural. [15]

What stage of "soft skill" versus "hard skill" learning are you at? Where do you want to be? What's stopping you? Do you spend enough time talking about and measuring the soft side of your business: relationship patterns; teachable moments; the integrity between staff, and between staff and customers?

EMPATHY A PEOPLE MATTER FOUNDATION

The promises we make to each other create islands of stability in the chaotic phases of leadership and organizational life. Our basic promise is to allow each other to be human and commit us to cleaning up the messes no one could foretell. It is crucial to recognize that moving forward with change is not a criticism of the past but, rather, recognition of positioning for the challenges of the future.

To be drawn to leadership work is to be drawn to the centre of the human condition—the eye of the storm. Leaders who are committed to change, but are without in-depth learning, are at risk of confusing the power of the organization with their own strength. When we speak of the world as it is, and what one can and cannot do, the leader helps others find their place. Strength stems from the possibilities and accomplishments of the collective, while humility stems from understanding and building relationships that establish strength. Together, these elements create an awakening within us.

Empathy is the ability to experience and relate to the thoughts, emotions, or experiences of others. For several years, research and work with leaders by the Centre for Creative Leadership (CCL) has shown that the nature of leadership is shifting, placing a greater emphasis on building and maintaining relationships. Leaders today need to be more person-focussed and able to work with those not just in the next cubicle but also with those in other buildings, or other states/provinces and countries.

Empathy is about putting yourself in another person's shoes. How do you correctly assess how they would feel in their shoes, not how you would feel in their shoes. Reflect on what we discussed in Chapter I: We share a basic dilemma and potential with barrier with everybody else, we live a rich life inside our heads.

Empathy is a leadership skill. Absent this skill ask yourself three questions: Can I truly predict the effect my decisions and actions will have? Can I build a team or nurture future leaders? Can I inspire followers or elicit loyalty?

In order to reinstate empathy, Entel and Grayson, the authors of *The Empathy Engine,* suggest a broad approach to customer service where all employees think about how they impact customer experience and relationships. The approach is anchored on the following three people-matter foundations:

TAP INTO THE INFORMAL

"Are you encouraging people to do the right thing when they see barriers to meeting patient needs? Have you provided them with guidance? What are you learning from today's workarounds? Are you spending time walking the halls and taking time to listen to employees? Are you demonstrating the empathy you want to see in your organizations?

STRENGTHEN THE FORMAL

"Are you explicit about the importance of empathy? Is it a criterion for hiring, rewards, and advancement? Have you identified the groups of current employees who have particularly strong service experience or inclination? Have you a plan to share best practices within your organizations?

HARMONIZE THE INFORMAL AND FORMAL

"Have you identified champions and what sets them apart? Do you share and cultivate those traits across your organizations? Do you encourage leaders and employees to tell stories of service to capture and spread? Do you engage in collaboration and experimentation to finds ways to keep your employees, including managers, close to the customer experience? [16]

Many organizations have discovered that empathy creates a holistic and focussed competitive advantage. They are able to sense customer problems and consistently act on them by keeping information and values flowing throughout. This form and flow of information includes key insights learned by front-line workers during their interactions with customers. The flow of values is an organizational commitment to empathy and customer service.

Bell Canada needed to make radical changes to many of its programs and processes to keep up with changes in the industry. As part of their turnaround plan, Bell looked to distinguish itself on customer service. Bell sought out the empathetic pride-builders of their organization—managers who were already demonstrating the desired behaviours they deemed characteristic of their new direction. Pride-builders were brought together to share best practices and to build on existing energy in the organization. A series of local performance-improvement pilots, driven by the best practices and energy of the pride-builders, yielded impressive customer-service results: Employee commitment, customer satisfaction, and sales all increased. Under strong senior leadership, pride-building became a "movement" with Bell Canada. "In the first three years of the effort, the informal community of pride-builders grew from ten initial groups of twelve to a thriving network of over 1,000 managers. The numbers clearly showcase the success of their chosen direction: a 29 percent increase in customer satisfaction, 10 percent increase in productivity and 13 percent increase in pride and motivation." [17]

Tapping existing sources of pride in an organization can build momentum and energy, and dramatically improve how an organization produces and delivers products and services. The greatest challenge in building respectful relationships is in the acknowledgment and acceptance of someone's struggles and differences. Understanding and progress requires an open mind; we must listen without judgment. This kind of relationship demonstrates respect by acceptance of one another on a platform that allows participants to be who they are, while holding each other fully responsible and accountable for their behaviour and communications.

When we are empathetic, we have the capacity to perceive the subjective experience of another person. We demonstrate empathy when we imagine another person's feelings, emotions, and sensitivities. We need to be willing to step into others' shoes in order to gain their perspective. To be empathetic, it is necessary to be self-aware. When we are self-aware, we are in touch with our own emotions, and therefore are able to read others' feelings. Empathy leads to quality relationships, integrity, trust, good communication, and values building.

Previously we talked about soft and hard skills, and impacts. Empathy involves scanning large human data sets, sorting out what's noise, and what's essential. As my grandfather counselled me: Ask, listen, talk, look through and around the obvious. When we let go, trust in others, and embrace external input, we are able to look around and through the obvious. To develop healthy relationships, a certain amount of openness and vulnerability is required. While it may not come naturally to all, moving out of our comfort zone can be very liberating. Being vulnerable does not mean we are walking around with a box of tissues sharing our deepest secrets with everyone. Being vulnerable at work simply means allowing ourselves to let our guard down, putting aside pretenses, and being our true selves. Being a vulnerable leader means being comfortable with not having all the answers, and wholeheartedly embracing the perspectives, opinions, and thoughts of others. Accepting vulnerability as an essential approach to leadership allows us to acknowledge our own flaws and current limitations.

It is deemed unprofessional to make mistakes. Failing to possess the right answer to a question within our area of expertise is viewed as an illustration of incompetence. In reality, not knowing does not equate to incompetence; it is completely human to err. Being a vulnerable leader means checking our misplaced egos at the door and becoming comfortable with not having all the answers. Our leadership influence grows proportionally to the number of people we surround ourselves with who complement our skills and bring the experience and wisdom necessary for creating new conversations and relationship patterns. Organizations are organic structures, patterns of human energy, and webs of relationships, conversations, and decisions between people. What keeps the patterns alive is the value placed on the people—the spirit and oxygen of organizations.

From my experiences, empathy is demonstrated by listening with curiosity and compassion. Empathy means moving beyond I hear what you are saying; it is about walking in others' shoes and signalling that you are part of this conversation to understand. While it may be uncomfortable, I learned that allowing for silence could contain tension, relief, or curiosity. My big learning was resisting the temptation, and at times pressure, to fill the vacuum because of my leadership role.

If the premise, "people matter, and relationships make the difference" is accepted, the totality and worth of an organization cannot be entirely expounded without the empathetic recognition and inclusion of its human value.

How is your leadership signalling that you are part of the conversation to understand?

LEVERAGING AND CONNECTING VALUES, PRINCIPLES, AND ETHICS

At the heart of all successful organizations is a set of core values the organization is passionate about. Values are the source of an organization's creative energy. The importance of protecting core values is highlighted in the research performed by the authors of *The Service Profit Chain*. The authors found that a distinguishing factor between high and low-performing organizations is their ability to adapt to a changing environment, whether it is legal, technological, social, or competitive. The authors believe the single most important indicator of adaptability is the adherence by management to a clear set of core values that stress the importance of delivering results to various constituencies, especially customers and employees. Their research provided three conclusions.

Three Distinguishing Features Between High and Low-Performing Organizations

1. Strong cultures don't win as consistently as adaptable ones

2. Adaptability is a result of the management mind being in accord with a set of core values that emphasize the importance of change; and

3. Organizations that vigorously practice core values and install devices for maintaining adaptability improve their chances of sustaining high performance over time and increase their chances of achieving successful transition from one leader to another. [18]

If we go to the highest good, to the vision of your organization, what question is implicit at its core? To illustrate, let's use this healthcare vision statement: "A healthcare system that keeps people healthy." Using this sample vision statement, we should ask: What is a healthcare system? How do we keep people healthy, and what does healthy mean? What is good care and how do we define it? How do we make our system sustainable for the future? Are those who implement strategy being driven by answers to these questions, or are they seeking their own answers? Extracting answers from these questions, we can begin to understand the value and culture attributes that could exist across all individuals and thereby create community.

Culture and values are not static, but rather a commitment to the condition of being. When the organization is coherent, little energy is wasted because of the internal synchronization among the parts. Increased coherence provides an emergence of creativity, innovation, cooperation, productivity, and quality on all levels. We must begin to bring more heart to what we do and make it safe for people to bring their own hearts into the workplace. Organizations need all the energy and passion they can muster. Engaging the heart means incorporating respect for the individual.

We as leaders should be challenged to walk the talk and demonstrate observable behaviours like earning respect by demonstrating trust, considering the interest and needs of others, respecting and treating others, as we want to be treated, seeking out and valuing viewpoints, and providing recognition.

Ultimately, our exhibited actions set a precedent and give others permission to conduct themselves in a similar fashion. It is imperative that we conduct ourselves in a manner that reflects the core values of our organizations and demonstrate our commitment to those in our organizations. Values, principles, and ethics are at the heart of successful leadership. Clarification and definition of values begins with a careful examination of deep-rooted beliefs and ideologies that guide an individual's actions and choices. Values represent the whole of a person; they reflect who a person is, what they are about, and their orientation to the world. They form the substance that ensures ethical consistency in conduct, and are generally motivated by a deep desire to do what is right by treating others with dignity and respect.

Leadership that is based on values is grounded in basic and constant moral guidelines, founded on the fundamental democratic value of inclusion, and rooted on the notion of mutual respect, acknowledging the legitimacy of competing diverse beliefs and values, and the creation of transcendent values that are shared by the leader and the team members. It embraces the belief that complexities associated with the world we live in today stem from uncertainty. Uncertainty is created from the inconsistencies in values between the leader and the followers.

Values manifest themselves in attitude and moral behaviour. People often draw assumptions about another person's values based on their own observations, and the personal experiences they have had with that specific individual. Declaration and disclosure of one's values can guide individual and collective conduct and resolve. This provides an opportunity to discover the similarities and differences at play. When value is understood, discord can be averted or resolved through dialogue.

Values determine the ethics we form and use to guide our lives. Our values and ethics form the morals that prompt our decisions. Values constitute "our personal bottom line, the ideals that give significance to our lives and are reflected through the priorities that we choose, and we act on consistently and repeatedly." Values serve as a private lamp or a beacon of light to guide the leader. Values are personal maps that emerge from our experiences, whereas principles represent natural laws that are an integral part of every enlightened society. People can share certain values, yet these values may be in conflict with fundamental principles—the enduring values. Our personal maps and values are more functional when they are congruent with principles or natural laws. Values define who we are, what we are, and what we stand for. We are exceedingly wise when we stand for something, because if we don't' stand for something, we will fall for anything.

Character ethic has a very strong linkage to values. The greatest American president said, "Character is like a tree, and reputation its shadow. The shadow is what we think of it; the tree is the real thing." [19]

Covey, in *Seven Habits of Successful People,* offers three resolutions by which leaders can attain core values, ethics, and principles. First, to overcome the restraining forces of appetites and passions, I resolve to exercise self-discipline and denial. Second, to overcome the restraining forces of pride and pretension, I resolve to work on character and competence. Third, to overcome the restraining forces of unbridled aspiration and ambition, I resolve to dedicate my talents and resources to noble purposes and to provide service to others." [20]

These resolutions lead to the inside-out notion of looking within to achieve leadership and personal potential. Covey suggests that the key to working from the inside out is to educate and obey the conscience. The best way to communicate values is through behaviour. We cannot become what we need to be by remaining what we are.

Societal norms, circumstance, and the people we associate with influence us. Greenleaf, in *Power of Servant Leadership,* provides a foundation for the subject of values-based leadership: "It begins with the natural feeling that one wants to serve, to serve first. Then conscious choice brings one to aspire to lead. The difference manifests itself in the care taken by the servant-first to make sure that other people's highest priority needs are being served. The best test is this: Do those served grow as persons; do they, while being served, become healthier, wiser, freer, more autono-mous, more likely themselves to become servants?" [21] Greenleaf wrote a dozen essays and books on servant-leadership. Briefly summarized, here are the critical characteristics:

Ten Critical Characteristics of Servant Leadership

1. *"Listening*: a deep commitment to listening intently to others

2. *Empathy*: people need to be accepted and recognized

3. *Healing:* one of the great strengths to heal oneself and others

4. *Awareness*: general awareness and self-awareness

5. *Persuasion*: reliance on persuasion, rather than positional authority

6. *Conceptualization:* thinking beyond day-to-day realities

7. *Foresight*: understand lessons from the past, realities of the present, and consequences of future

8. *Stewardship*: holding their institutions in trust for the greater good of society

9. *Commitment*: to the growth of people and a learning organization

10. *Building community*: living in and with the full community."[21]

Value, principles and ethics guide the development of relationship patterns. We need to understand our values and the values held by those we work with. For any form of transformation to occur within an organization, and (more specifically) in order for it to flourish, a great measure of mindfulness must be placed upon the diversity of people that make up the organization.

What's your leadership role in creating and honouring values, principles and ethics?

DIVERSITY OF THINKING
AND INCLUSION

How can leaders and organizations reinvent the standard of diversity of thinking and inclusion and truly lead without embracing and valuing differences? From the writings of Paulo Coelho: "I have met so many people who, at first opportunity, try to show their worst qualities. They hide their inner strength behind aggression and hide their insecurity behind an air of independence. They do not believe in their own abilities but are constantly trumpeting their virtues. I read these messages in many I meet. I am never taken in by appearances and make a point of remaining silent when people try to impress me. I use these occasions to correct my own faults, for other people make an excellent mirror. I use every opportunity to teach myself." [22]

His message tells us to lead and inspire by example, by personifying the qualities of honesty, integrity, diversity, resilience, and confidence, and demonstrates how leadership is a process of self-development, not an ultimate arrival.

We cannot elevate others to a higher purpose until we have first elevated ourselves. We cannot lead others until we have first led ourselves through a struggle with opposing values. A leader with integrity has one self, which is the same at home and at work, with family and with colleagues. Such a leader has a unifying set of values that guide choices of action regardless of the situation. We must step out into the unknown and begin with the exploration of our inner-territory. Using this as our base, we can discover and unleash the leader within.

Progressive diversity is the product of bringing together individuals who appear different but have common characteristics on a deep level. The notion of focusing on similarities and acknowledging the differences may serve as a strategy for positive change. An organization's commitment to diversity is visible through the manner in which it creates and maintains its culture. The manner in which individual members are viewed and treated projects the character of the organization and its collective leadership. Dignity, respect, and worth are paramount to communicating corporate commitment to diversity.

To build and sustain healthy learning organizations, we must create respectful relationships built on an inclusive sentiment. People have different predilections and beliefs based on natural-born preferences and their life experiences. Each person looks at the world through a set of lenses formed by personal biases and their interaction with the system in which they function. This dissimilarity will influence the dynamics and outcomes of all human interactions. Hayles and Mendez Russell, in *The Diversity Directive*, provide an explanation and foundation for diversity of thinking and inclusion:

Eight Foundations for Progressive Diversity

1. "Personal diversity work involves head, hand, and heart – what we know, do, and feel.

2. Doing diversity work increases personal and professional effectiveness.

3. Group or team synergies are made possible by member diversity.

4. Organizations that maintain and value diversity are less likely to make business blunders caused by not understanding their markets, customers, or clients.

5. Diverse teams tend to outperform homogeneous teams, especially on complex tasks.

---

6. Organizations that conduct effective diversity work are measurably more productive and profitable.

7. Individuals who do not accept the research-based business case for diversity are probably emotionally opposed and may respond more favourably to emotional appeals.

8. Pull, don't push, to win participants for diversity work."[23]

Fostering a vision for a work culture that emphasizes diversity of thinking and inclusion is an organizational imperative. The formation of a vision is often motivated by a keen desire to leave a legacy or fulfill a dream. Visions are generated based on the assumption that anything is possible. Visions are not restricted by attainability or feasibility. Idealism prevails because visions are expressions of hope and optimism.

Leaders must exhibit an inexhaustible passion for their vision. This requires the demonstration and application of emotion and enthusiasm at every opportunity. A vision differentiates one organization from another. It serves to motivate individuals to work collectively toward a common goal and helps to foster pride. Kouzes and Posner, in *The Leadership Challenge*, state: "The most important role of visions in organizational life is to give focus to human energy. Visions are like lenses that focus un-refracted rays of light."[24]

To enable everyone concerned with the enterprise to see more clearly what's ahead of them, leaders must have and convey focus and finish. All priorities and efforts should be aligned when they are guided by a shared vision. It reflects an ultimate state based on shared ideals. These ideals resonate in core assumptions about people and the world that we live in. People from all parts need to come together to create a powerful vision that builds the kind of organization we wish to see.

Leaders in this environment need to be continuous learners, who share an intuitive emotional and personal identity with the organization. Such human resolve is how organizations came about. It is with this same human resolve that they will outgrow current challenges.

The more leaders generate a diversity of interpretations and the more different pieces of the puzzle are laid out on the table the better equipped you are to generate necessary human system interventions. A shared vision of diversity of thinking and inclusion that is honoured each day places partners at the same table with a common goal. The organization's vision must therefore be fostered and followed at all levels so that it becomes entrenched in culture. By marshalling our diverse resources, we can create powerful coalitions.

The challenge is to invite people to come forward with their ideas, to encourage them to take a risk and share their knowledge. What are you doing to create a vision of cultural diversity?

CULTURE EATS STRATEGY FOR BREAKFAST

The word "culture" is derived from the word for agricultural cultivation. Cultivation of the soil to produce requires time and attention, nurturing, shelter and protection, patience, understanding, and preparedness for environmental changes. Building a culture takes work; it is about incremental relationship building with people.

Shawn Parr in a Fast Company article suggests culture, like brand is misunderstood and often discounted as a touchy-feely component that belongs to HR. It's not intangible or fluffy. It's one of the most important drivers to organizational success. With regards to organizational vibrancy and success Parr asks a number of questions.

"In your organizational activities, do you run into your culture every day? When you reflect on your organizational and departmental culture, does it inspire you, or smack you in the face and get in your way, slowing and wearing you down? Does your culture overpower or does it inspire you to overcome current and future organizational people and relationship challenges?

Are you spending important time to understand what is driving your culture? Is it power and ego that people react to, and try to gain power, or a culture of encouragement and empowerment? As previously discussed, how healthy are your organizational space conditions? Are the organizational space conditions driven from top-down directives, or cross-department collaboration?

To get a taste of your culture, all you have to do is sit in an executive meeting, the cafe or the lunch room, listen to the conversations, look at the way decisions are made and the way departments cooperate. Take time out and get a good read on the health of your culture."[25]

Regardless of our leadership role, we are working within various forms of hierarchy and culture, side to side, up and down the chains of command and organizational spaces. A learning culture consisting of openness, trust, engaged workforce, and an aligned vision creates a culture committed to continuous improvement. Corporate culture reflects the adopted philosophy, principles, and practices for the treatment of people and conduct of business. As we've discussed, culture is expressed as vision, values, guiding principles, and policy framework. To a large extent, organizational culture is shaped and maintained by leaders as they set the stage for expected behaviour.

Covey defined culture as "a pattern of shared basic assumptions that the group learned as it solved its problems of external adaptation and internal integration, that has worked well enough to be considered valid, and therefore, to be taught to new members as the correct way to perceive, think, and feel in relation to those problems."[20] Culture and leadership are interdependent. Understanding the dynamics of culture is important for everyone and essential for leaders. Culture originates from three primary sources: beliefs, values, and assumptions of the founders of organizations; learning experiences of group members as their organization evolves; and new beliefs, values, and assumptions brought in by new members and leaders.

It is important for organizations to declare their desired culture. Their declaration helps clarify the core principles that are to guide the behaviour and actions of everyone within that organization. Instilling parameters and expectations, and clearly indicating consequences of non-compliance, can prevent confusion and inappropriate conduct. As leaders, we are responsible for institutionalizing expected behaviours and intervening when deviations are observed. If we fail to address deviations in a timely manner, the unintended result is sabotage.

As organizations mature, cultural dynamics become increasingly complex, because parts of the organization will tend to create their own sub-cultures. The key is to develop and sustain a corporate culture and integrate across existing sub-cultures. Our personal values, principles, and ethics must align with those of the organization. Failure to achieve congruence between leadership and self can result in poor morale, mistrust, and cynicism. This alignment between individual and corporate values is important at all levels of the organization. The role and actions of the leader contributes to the collective mind of an organization.

The hallmarks of a leading and learning organization are strong people-focussed cultures, with a compelling vision of the organization as a great place for both customers and staff, and a spirit of sharing ideas for doing things better. Leadership must be rooted in this culture in order to formulate authentic and successful relations. Leaders need to have the courage and conviction to create highly participatory cultures that enables them, and others, to achieve their maximum potential.

An assumption of human systems is that the knowledge and wisdom on how to change the system is within the system itself. As discussed in Chapter I, for top, middle and bottom spaces, the focus of organizational systems should be on the spaces between the boxes, between the component parts of the organizational system. Simple recipes won't work. A primary leadership focus should be: relationships, relationships, relationships … rather than on the machine-like functions. People need to be free to unleash their capacity to transform the present to a future focus.

Interaction and participation are unavoidable in human organizations and it is from these patterns of interaction and participation that organizational configurations and cultures emerge. These configurations are not cast in stone. Too often we blame the system or the culture as the culprit when our plans fail. The fault lies in the processes of conversation. Human beings and the patterns of their participation and interaction create culture, and, if you like, the organizational system. Culture is an emergent property of an organization and as such the humans who created can change it. L. Ledoux provides four cultural and structural observation points that leaders should continually pay attention to.

THE PAST TRAPS THE FUTURE

"Over time, the structures, culture, and defaults that make up an organizational system become deeply ingrained, self-reinforcing, and very difficult to reshape. Many organizations get trapped by their current ways of doing things, simply because these ways worked in the past.

FORMAL STRUCTURES

An organization's formal structures create the playing field and rules for all activities that take place in the overarching system. For example, structures may reward certain behaviors or attitudes (such as not making mistakes or bringing in new business or customer satisfaction) and implicitly discourage other behaviors and attitudes (risk taking or increasing business from existing clients or focusing on improving employee morale).

FOLKLORE

An organization's culture is made up of its folklore (the stories that people frequently tell that indicate what is most important), its rituals (such as how new employees are welcomed into the company), its group norms (including styles of deference and dress codes), and its meeting protocols (like modes of problem solving and decision making). All of these cultural ingredients influence the organization's adaptability. Unlike structures, the culture of an organization is not usually written down or formally documented, so it may be hard to describe in precise terms. But like structures, culture still powerfully determines what is considered acceptable and unacceptable behavior.

DEFAULTS

In addition to structures and culture, an organization's problem-solving defaults can provide insights into the way your organization operates as a system – and its adaptability. Defaults are the ways of looking at situations that lead people to behave in ways that are comfortable and that have generated because they are familiar and they have proved useful for explaining reality and solving problems in the past. A default interpretation, leading to a default response, puts people on familiar ground and plays to their organization's strengths. But in several respects, it can also be a constraint. It can blind people."[26]

As a leader what is your role in creating a vibrant culture?

MOVING FORWARD

Many employees feel they have ended up in workplaces that see them as cogs in machines; disposable and little value. They are unclear of the present and fear the future.

A primary task of leadership should be to develop the organization's most critical asset: its dedicated and caring people. As previously mentioned, the overall success of an organization is not established merely by the completion of tasks or the agendas laid forth, but through the motivation and dedication of its people. The level of devotion is founded on, and fluctuated by, feelings of inclusion, recognition, ability to contribute, and opportunity for growth. When people feel voiceless or insignificant, every other aspect of them tends to mirror that feeling of vulnerability.

Hope sees the invisible, feels the intangible, and achieves the impossible. As a leader you have either a legal or moral authority to demand a wave of organizational improvement and promote new opportunities to improve the customer experience.

Credible leaders model the values and purpose of the organization. High-performing organizations reflect these values and its purpose at all levels. People in such organizations feel free to speak up and identify conflict/disconnects/inconsistencies. Everyone shares accountability for achieving the organizational purpose and is imbued with the personal authority to take action.

It is up to today's leaders to lead with integrity, to model the values and purpose of the organization in every aspect of their work, and to encourage such behaviour at all levels of the organization.

Let's Imagine Five Perspectives:

1. *New Customer-Driven Perspective.* Imagine an emphasis on seamless customer experiences, the elimination of gaps, and consistent quality standards. Imagine an improvement in customer satisfaction while holding costs down. Imagine honest conversations about outcome variances.

2. *New Culture Perspective.* Imagine passion, pride, hope, commitment, respect, trust, confidence, participation, abundance mindset, and high morale instilled within all employees. Imagine a prevailing curiosity concerning what we know and what we don't know.

3. *New Skills and Capacity Perspective.* Imagine strategic execution, system-thinking skills, team learning, collective intelligence, and problem solving. Imagine a knowledge base of evidence derived from processes and outcomes. Imagine honed collaboration skills for achieving outcomes. Imagine a common language framework for talking about, planning for, and implementing change.

4. *New Structural and Value-Creating Perspectives.* Imagine interdependent versus former independent organizational spaces focussed on the needs of the common customers.

5. *New Resources Perspective.* Imagine a leveraged use of human and fiscal resources, evidence-based decision-making, transparency, and strategic oversight.

REFLECTIONS AND CONSIDERATIONS

It is up to today's leaders to lead with integrity, to model the values and purpose of the organization in every aspect of their work, and to encourage such behaviour at all levels of the organization. How do you judge how well you are living up to your responsibility to live out the values and purpose of the organization?

Great leaders place emphasis on the success of those around them and their own personal performance. How often do you extend your efforts to help someone else succeed? What opportunities for growth and learning do you provide? A great indicator of valuable leadership is the level and quality of leadership components instilled in the people they lead.

A vital responsibility of leaders is to develop the next generation of leaders. Are your leadership developments trickling down and being absorbed by your team? Are you receiving anything from your efforts?

Trust is an integral aspect of leadership. When you reflect on your leadership style, behaviour, action, and talk, are you elevating a level of trust in those around you? How do you gauge the present level of trust? How can you tap into and create a culture that encourages the expression of intellect, passion, commitment, and experience by all levels of the delivery system? How can you create a culture that encourages cohesive future? How can you lead the development of a cohesive system that satisfies consumer needs and expectations?

Your organization has people gifts you require to move forward. How are you tapping into it? Every individual has the capacity to contribute to organizational transformation. What are you doing to nurture it? How can an organization achieve the right balance of authority, autonomy, and accountability, so that it can achieve measurable improvements over the next three to five years?

How does an organization grow if its employees do not? What if the leadership that employs them cripples their learning potential? Whose job is it to fix it? What code of conduct must the executive create, and model, that will show everyone the rewards of making it work? The learning-organization metaphor is a powerful tool, but how do you develop it practically? What behaviour have you tolerated in yourself, or in others, that can no longer be tolerated?

Do you agree with the following statement? "All the information you require to learn from each other is always present. To learn from others, much of what you need to know is within you, right here and now."[27]

CHAPTER III
ORGANIZATIONAL ELASTICITY AND EFFECTIVENESS

"Coming together is a beginning; keeping together
is progress; working together is success."
~ Henry Ford

INTRODUCTION

Humanizing Leadership creates the glue that holds the fabric of a human system together, and the elasticity, bond, and effectiveness of the glue is determined by the overall relationship welfare of the organization. Organizations do not exist of fragmented parts, but rather of a series of human systems within a larger human system.

In Chapter III we begin with a simple truth: what goes on between people defines what an organization is and what it can become. We discuss the reality in which you operate in as a living and complex human system of multi-dimensional relationships.

I ask what would happen if leaders spent part of their time being engaged where work and services are actually performed and delivered. From here we discuss how every organization is made up of interconnecting circles of activities and learning patterns and yet we are conditioned to see and think in straight lines. I discuss how new mindsets based on a human-system perspective are key leadership and relationship development foundations. I end with some liberation and authenticity insights.

MULTI-DIMENSIONAL RELATIONSHIPS AND EXTERNAL CONDITIONS

Elasticity and effectiveness of the organizational glue is determined by the overall relationship welfare of the organization. Relationships create and define organizations. Human system relationships present the third element of organizational design. We are certainly aware that structure follows strategy and function follows form. We are also seeing that relationships run the show, and without relationships there is no strategy implementation, there is no function to begin with.

From my experience, organizations and change initiatives that emphasize quality of relationships are in a better position to leverage their collective knowledge for long-term sustainability. Whether it is creating a product, delivering a service, or negotiating a partnership, organizations are an aggregation of endless formal and informal interactions. The most effective leaders are able to draw on the capabilities, expertise, and different perspectives within their informal networks. The importance of relationships can also be found in an organization's external interactions, where a range of stakeholders, customers, suppliers, shareholders, employers, and communities in which an organization is based play a role in success or failure.

At the root of "relationships" is the discipline of a learning organization. Learning organizations invest in the education and growth of their people so that they have the internal capacity to achieve their organization's vision with focused, well-executed strategies that leverage resources and mobilize people to achieve the results required. Peter Senge, in *The Fifth Discipline*, believes that building a learning organization requires basic shifts in how we think and interact. The journey involves an exercise in personal commitment to being open to learning. Without communities of people who are genuinely committed to learning together, there is no real chance of moving forward.

True learning organizations have the ability to perceive and evaluate the tacit depths of an organizational and departmental environment "within a nanosecond." This is an empathetic skill. It requires one to be present in the moment and access the stillness from which organizational identity arises, and to perceive the effect of relationship patterns.

R. Short suggests, "What goes on between people defines what an organization is and what it will become. Think about the reality the idea introduces. You are no longer just an individual, but an individual standing in the middle of many relationships. For example, nobody can be a customer without a supplier and a relationship. The systems are you, the others, and your relationships. Much of what you once thought of as independent actions are now people transactions and transitions. You are now positioned to notice not just yourself and other individuals, but the dance that happens between and among you. The genetic code of an organization is embedded in thousands of interactions that occur every day between people everywhere in the organization, and relationships are the heart and soul of an organization; how we utilize and nurture these relationships has a profound impact on organizational outcomes."[1]

Companies such as Starbucks, Virgin and Nike, have clearly and inventively demonstrated the market value of customer relationships in business. Let us take a moment to define what is intended when we speak of relationships. Relationships are the way in which two or more people regard and behave toward each other, or the way in which two or more people are connected. Healthy relationships are multi-dimensional. People in human organizational systems relate to each other as individuals, role holders, same discipline colleagues, inter-professional colleagues, technical supports, functional supports customers, suppliers etc.

The environment and reality in which you operate is a living and complex human system that requires open-systems thinking. Organizations do not exist of fragmented parts, but rather a series of human systems within a human system. This requires considerable transformation in traditional approaches to relationships. It demands a more collaborative and participatory approach; one that engages the whole organization.

As discussed in Chapter I, the real power within an organization is not present in the definition of the organizational box, or the tasks, or a separate department mission and vision to support the overall company mission and vision. The real power is in the relationship between the individuals and with the organization as a whole. This relationship power can be positive or negative. It is easy to see negative relationships between individuals and departments that result in barriers to success and/or even sabotage within the company. It is a little hard to see and build positive relationships when the leader does not get off the top pedestal and find out what is actually happening on the ground. Often the charts we discussed earlier depicting top down heroic leadership have a tendency and vulnerability to create the feeling of "disconnectedness" between people working in the middle and bottom spaces.

To overcome this phenomenon, it will be necessary to de-emphasize the power of the organizational chart and instead focus on the power of the relationship. Organizational power is totally relational and relationship based. Truly powerful organizations develop strong internal and external relationships. Once a positive relationship is established, power is created. Think about statements we have all heard before: "All of us are smarter than one of us" and "the whole is greater than the sum of its parts."

For any organization, the environment consists of the set of external conditions and forces that have the potential to influence the organization. It is useful to break the concept of the environment down into two components. The general environment (or macro environment) includes overall trends and events in society, such as social trends, technological trends, demographics, and economic conditions. The industry (or competitive environment) consists of multiple organizations that collectively compete with one another by providing similar goods, services, or both. Ditton and Macleod, in an essay titled "Health System Relationships: A Paradigm Shift", describe three elements of multidimensional relationships.

TRENDS IN SOCIETY IMPACTING ON ORGANIZATIONS

"Two major cultural trends of the 21st Century are individualism and economic rationalism. Both of these trends have been greatly influenced by technology. Individualism fosters a climate of 'independence.' It is an ideology founded on the principal of "me" rather than "other." Individualism impacts the development of organizations and workplaces. The level of trust between employees has a significant impact on their health, well-being and work performance.

Economic rationalism is a form of ideological reasoning and is based on the notion that the free market is a much better arbiter of economics and other matters than the governments that are in place. Economic rationalism is a science largely devoid of social goals, and the language and logic of economics begins to dominate social policy. A corollary of such reasoning is a reduction in spending by the governments on things such as education, health and social welfare, along with a shift of public services to the private realm.

Cultural trends and underlying themes of individualism and economic rationalism challenge, and impact social capital. Technology is now heavily integrated into modern life and shapes many cultural dimensions. It operates as part of the socio-economic, cultural and environmental condition. Embracing and understanding organizational relationships will create new conversations. The underlying theme of the mediocrity, and the process of networking for political power versus the value of learning and improving through critical reflection with teams and systems, can be surfaced.

VERTICAL, HORIZONTAL, LONGITUDINAL, AND CIRCULAR RELATIONSHIPS

Leaders are subjected to many types of relationships. First, chain of command-controlled relationship vertically directed down from CEO to the front-line. These relationships are bound by rules and regulations, and maintained by the employment contract and psychological contract between employer and employee. Second, horizontal relationships are those with peers, fellow workers in the day-to-day routines. Third, longitudinal relationships deal with the reality of changes in relationships as peers, superiors and subordinates come and go from the workplace over time. Fourth, the notion of circular relationships refers to those relational interactions that have a feedback loop in them. All these relationships operate within single disciplines and across disciplines.

RELATIONSHIPS DO NOT RUN SMOOTHLY

It is a truism to say relationships do not run smoothly. In organizations what we want to know is how to prepare those work relationships to anticipate, prevent and manage our organizational challenges. By way of risk literature, we need to walk in the other person's shoes for a while to see what they see, to understand work from their perspective. Understanding an experience from the other perspective makes it easier to reduce difficulties. For example, understanding the impact of forced overtime over an extended period of time. The effects of stress and fatigue encountered, and with it the increased possibility of error, must not only be recognized but also acknowledged and resolved. By understanding other people's experiences, we are provided with the knowledge necessary to produce alternative working arrangements."[2]

In this rich tapestry of relationship patterns, cycles of connectivity are established between people, and micro systems can develop where excellence flourishes. So too, patterns of avoidance and lack of mindfulness can develop. Team functioning contains a paradox: the group work is better than the sum of individual effort, while at the same time the group is vulnerable to the weakest member of the team. Do you agree?

GOING TO THE DANCE FLOOR

We often talk about how we seek meaning in our work. Meaning is not extracted from books or videos on learning and leadership. It comes from within and is reinforced through our relationship interactions with others. Organizations have a soul, a spirit, something that is outside of your organizational structure and systems. When you go into a well-functioning organizational unit, you can feel it. Anybody can feel it. You walk into an organizational space, and you say, "There is enthusiasm here; there is energy here. People like to work in this place, people believe in this place."

If we were to walk through a pair of medical wards, high-school classrooms, fast-food outlets, or retail chain stores, there is good chance they would feel differently. Regardless of processes and activity, one could impart a sense of harmony while the other yields a sense of tension and disconnect. Each pair offers the same layout, staff profiles, and IT system and procedures, but there is something perceptibly different. Unfortunately, the ambitions, ideals, skills, and talents at the social and cultural core of an organization often experience a profound daily affront to its sense of competency and greatness.

What would happen if we spent a significant part of our time being engaged in the space where services are actually delivered? Some organizations, especially those adopting lean management systems, are doing this and finding it dramatically changes their understanding of how human systems work and what needs to change. It also puts the power and responsibility for continuous improvement in the hands of those who actually deliver services. This changes our role as a leader, where we become a coach and supporter.

This is a radical change for most organizations and a substantial transition for a leader to go through. A leader must depart from being a knowledge expert and become a visible and present leader whose greatest skill is asking the right questions. Through repositioning, they can better understand the dynamics of the organizational white space as well as the connections between the top, middle, and bottom spaces.

Many leaders would confess that they are not comfortable being close to the point of service delivery they oversee. When is the last time a hospital CEO put on greens and spent time in an operating room? When did the manufacturing company vice president responsible for materials management spend time in the warehouse understanding that process? When did the retail sales general manager spend time as a customer to understand the value of relationships and people? How often do we spend time in areas that are not our direct responsibility or participate in quality improvement initiatives outside our personal portfolio? I wonder what we would learn if this became our norm? A hypothesis: all the information required for transformation and improvement is always present within human-system spaces.

For a moment, let's elevate high above the organizational dance floor to a height where we can observe all its activity. The music will be inaudible from our vantage point but there are particulars we can count on. There will be numerous records played that chronicle the protocols, agendas, and missions of government and the CEO in charge. Records that upper-and-middle management select and spin based on need. The records in the collection stem back decades and are continually updated. Every new transformational-change initiative and every new or updated leadership development framework is pressed onto a record and released for immediate airplay.

We quickly spot the instructors below. Each is responsible for teaching the membership the new dance of the week, month, or year. Their job is to get all participants to move in synch with the music, to follow a sequence of steps. It is obvious from the start that some of the instructors seem unprepared, confused, or in some cases possibly unqualified. Their role is to lead; yet their direction and explanations appear muddled. Proper dance execution requires quick and lively movements, yet there seems to be a lot of reactionary steps—steps out of line with the music.

On the other hand, some of the participants have caught on to the new dance quickly; their tempo and steps are on point. It is not clear if their proficiency stems from their optimism, belief in the new dance, or their keen desire to adapt and excel. Others look to be distracted or even annoyed; it looks like they preferred the music that was played a while back. They are frustrated and waiting for the music to switch back over to the sound of time past. These individuals knew the old routine well and their place in it. This group, with their arms crossed, does not seem willing to change.

It appears there are some participants tapping their feet on the periphery of the dance floor, unsure whether to join the action or stay back like a wallflower. These people may need some added encouragement. We can count on them falling in line, though, once the majority of the participants hit their stride. They will eventually follow the lead.

We can witness others looking around, searching for someone to express their confusion and concerns to, but they seem unable to find the right source. They look like they are ready to give up.

It becomes evident, the longer we watch the orchestration on the dance floor, that this is not a regimented dance. Perhaps the music is being played at too high an rpm. Maybe the dance is much too technical for the group to embrace and master. Maybe the music, DJ, and instructors are completely out of synch.

We know there was an execution plan; executive directors were supposed to teach the strategic-dance plan to the dance instructors. The dance instructors were supposed to teach the strategic-dance plan to the dancers. So, what happened? Maybe if we weren't so far away from the dance floor we could have participated. We could have received feedback and helped with the orchestration of the dance. We could have at least demonstrated our own participation and buy in. Maybe the dance was coming from the wrong source.

Otto Scharmer, author, thought leader, and senior lecturer at MIT Sloan School of Management, suggests that we live in an age of profound disruptions. He sees a solution that begins between our ears. "The ultimate goal is to live in harmony with a deep sense of appreciation for, and commitment to, others through nurtured relationships. This cannot be realized unless there is a strong sense of self-worth and knowledge of self. If one believes in diversity then one must also demonstrate a visible commitment to creating an ideal society—living in community." [3]

As discussed previously, the essence of an organization is relationships. "We are now positioned to notice ourselves, other individuals, and the dance that happens between and amongst us. If we change our part in the dance we change our organization." [1]

Are you changing your part in the dance? How?

CIRCLES OF CONNECTIVITY
AND PATTERNS OF ENERGY

Every organization is made up of interconnecting circles of complex activity. Yet people are conditioned to see dots on a map and think in straight lines. In an essay titled "A Last Word from the Balcony of Personal Reflection," I made the following observations: "The multiplicity of professionals within complex organizational hierarchies present challenges, but they do in other systems and structures as well. There is ample transformational insight to be gained from nature itself. For instance, a flower garden consists of flowers that vary in colour, size, shape, height, texture, and smell. They perform varied functions in the ecosystem, but if we examine underground we find, at their foundation level, the roots are all interconnected. If we look more closely, we see the flowers are held up by a structure of stems that reach from the shadow of the earth to the light of day. What we do not see is the real source of structural integrity: the root systems hidden below the surface of the soil.

How does this relate to your organization and its systems? The flower garden is like the formal structure of an organization; it is a containing vessel. If the content, the actual culture itself, is not provided with the proper nourishment, the contents will decay or at best produce mediocre results. Without proper maintenance, the flowerbed will grow in every direction and out of control. All future growth will be left to chance. If the foundation of the vessel is neglected, the entire system will collapse."[4] To enable the natural 'organic' elements of an organization to foster change, sustenance must be on offer. If organizations and systems are a living human system—ecology of overlapping, interpenetrating relational spheres—then leadership may be defined as shaping 'life-enhancing' conditions.

Complexity theorists argue that an emergence of order within a system is not a magical phenomenon; it involves tending and encouragement from its component agents. Through a process of tending and encouragement, organizations will evolve. We will leave behind the historical patterns of silo organizations and command-control hierarchies. At the organizational level, management becomes focused on self-management in a team setting. Articulation is far easier than implementation. This is often referred to as the "knowing-doing gap." We all know more than we need to about achieving outcomes. It is imperative that we transform what we know into what we do. To paraphrase Margaret Wheatley in *Finding Our Way*, when the system is struggling, bring the components together so it can learn about itself from itself. Our organizations have all the gifts needed to move forward. We must take action to harness and nurture the growth of those integral individuals that enable a connected human system to emerge and flourish.

Patterns of Energy

As we discussed earlier, organizations are patterns of energy, webs of human relationships, conversations, and decisions. Relationships and interactions are the 'genetic code' of organizations. Think about this reality: Employees are not just individuals but rather individuals standing in the middle of many relationship systems. As a leader, when we change our part of the relationship pattern, we change the organization. Change requires a shift. Relationships do not change unless leaders and the individuals with whom they interface change their interactions and understanding.

An empowering skill is the ability to look within and to gain awareness of the origins of first reaction(s). To realize that we create the impact others have on us is, without a doubt, one of the most difficult and important leadership lessons to learn. We need to increase our awareness, along with our range of informed choices. Awareness is using the available choices to create differentiated learning relationships. We may wake up one day and realize that our learning grows when we make here-and-now choices differently.

Unfortunately, it is far more typical for individuals or teams to want others to change first. Individuals and teams wait for it to be safe and risk-free before they step outside their comfort zone and participate. This process is absent of growth, learning, and awareness because everyone waits on someone else to act.

Based on moments of personal reflection, we as leaders can undertake our key responsibility, which is to create the systemic conditions within the organization that provide solutions to today's challenges. Leaders foster conditions in which systems can outgrow constraints and current approaches. "If leadership requires followship, is leadership a shift from managing others to managing yourself with others?' Is leadership operating from the inside out through the observations of the motives, intentions, feelings, judgments, and attributes that drive our responses to others?" [1]

Can labels like 'organization' or 'system' get in the way? "For many people, these labels conjure up images and assumptions of an entity that exists out there in time and space, a legal abstraction that exists somewhere distant from the individuals who make up its essence. An organization or system is not something abstract that floats around in space, separate from those who come to work every day to deliver care. Any effort to improve relationships begins with us, the leader." [1]

Change requires a literal opening and emptying, an event that creates space for a new vision to emerge, a vision that articulates shared values. To approach this opening requires discipline and courage. We need discipline to look at what is not working and to resist knee-jerk reactions to new ideas, and the courage to detach from old patterns, structures, and processes, which are no longer useful to an evolving organizational system.

Rather than thinking and acting as isolated silos under siege, governance and managerial leaders can choose to see themselves through another lens—to view themselves and their organizations in a relationship. When we examine the held assumptions regarding what exists today and what the future holds, we are able to create new conversations and opportunities. Assumptions are not facts; they are currently held beliefs about our reality and our vision. The first assumption that system leaders need to test is whether they have all the questions to the challenges and dilemmas they face.

We know that people are capable of brilliance. The answers to the dilemmas we face are within our own organizations.

How are you discovering what gets in the way? What are you going to change?

PERSONAL INSIGHTS
FROM HOME

Recently, my wife and I were involved in a major home renovation. Keeping a watchful eye, we quickly observed variables that altered the progress, execution, and quality of work performed. Although all trade people are certified to perform their job, we observed that not all individuals perform their job to the same level of care and attention. Perhaps it was their individual work ethic that determines outcome; maybe it was the program, apprenticeship, or company they worked for that hinders their ability. Maybe they were wrapped up in personal problems outside of work, unable to separate their personal life from their business life. Or maybe it was fatigue; they have worked too many consecutive days, and the long hours are leading to burn out. Perhaps they had hoped for an easy job rather than a complicated one.

Extending beyond the individual worker, maybe the trade person has a personal conflict with their boss, or general contractor. Maybe it is the incompetence of the general contractor and their inability to orchestrate the project. Maybe the tools had an affect on outcome or the new techniques and technologies they have yet to master. Maybe some individuals on the project were working towards professional advancement, while others were complacent with where they are. Maybe some contractors looked for shortcuts, while others were consumed by perfectionism.

We realized how the harmony between and amongst the crew had a significant impact on the quality of the outcome. We also recognized that when the crew upholds a high standard, performance is elevated to achieve that held expectation.

Ultimately, we learned that we have little control over execution, attitude, behaviours, skills, pride, deadlines, and completion timelines. We witnessed firsthand that trade apprenticeship-development programs resulting in trade certifications did not guarantee quality, attitude, pride, and customer service. On sequencing and handoffs between framing, plumbing, electrical, drywall, finishing, and painting, we witnessed how one profession could hold others up and professional rivalry, pettiness, and blaming occurs. We learned that not all these individuals possessed the ability to articulate the problems and solutions and progress with absolute clarity and conviction.

The following story of the three brick masons illustrates different levels of attitude and passion: Three brick masons were working together on a project. The first was asked what is being built, and the answer was gruffly presented: "I'm laying bricks." The second brick mason was then asked the same question. Reply was, "I'm building a wall." The third brick mason was asked the same question. Looking up, and with great enthusiasm and pride, said, "I'm building a cathedral."

J. Dykstra's leadership blog on intent, action, and effect says, "If you search for this story online you'll find many different variations, most including some sort of explanation about how the tale speaks to a person's attitude and ability to see the big picture. While these things are true and insightful, this story makes me wonder about something else. Why is it that some companies seem to have an overwhelming amount of cathedral-builders? On the other hand, why do other businesses seem to contain hordes of bricklayers?"[5]

There is no question that a person's individual perspective (attitude, ability to see the big picture, etc.) is crucial, but the importance of the culture that individual is apart of is often highly underestimated. If there is a "we" component to our work, if there is something about the collective group that makes us either better or worse as individuals, then this story isn't just about a person's mindset. It's also about the culture surrounding the person.

As leaders, we have very little direct control over how other people think, but if there's something about the environment a person is in that creates either more or less meaning in their work, then leaders are on the hook for something different. A work environment, unlike a person's outlook, is something a leader has a huge amount of control over.

As a leader, how are you creating more cathedral-builders and learning environments in your organizations?

Do you recognize any commonalities between what is going on in your organization and this quick overview of a home renovation?

MINDSETS

Forward-thinking organizations are preparing for what the next few years will throw at them, and leadership is often touted as what will help weather the storm. This logic is not wrong; in fact, it's right. However, leadership doesn't depend on a few skills or even many skills. Leadership is more than a skill; it's a mindset that shapes everything we do.

Before we look at a leadership mindset, let's take a look at why focusing on leadership skills alone doesn't work. The leadership skills provided in a development program often do not have the desired effect back in the workplace. Skills development works well in fields that have specific and unchanging rules to learn. In the current business climate, even if we think there are 'rules,' they are changing too rapidly for us to keep up with. Leadership models, tools, and techniques have a short shelf life outside the training room. When we try these skills out in projects, or on our real-life colleagues, they fall short.

Teams might be trying out new leadership behaviours, but in order for these behaviours to stick, we need a different leadership mindset—a different way of thinking. Without the proper mindset, any new leadership skills will fail to sit right, and therefore are less likely to have long-term staying power. In short, leadership-skills training provides a model to follow, when in reality, we know leadership does not work like that. This observation from the Thor leadership blog sums it up nicely: "Focusing on a leadership mindset forces us to look at how we think about ourselves and relate to the world, and spotlights current behaviours and their effects. Developing a leadership mindset requires us to start practicing new behaviours, and those behaviours feel like they 'fit' because they're borne out of a way of thinking and not a skills model or technique."[6]

In a 2014, Mckinsey & Company wrote a report titled "Why Leadership Development Programs Fail." The authors talked with hundreds of chief executives about the leadership-development struggle, observing both successful initiatives and ones that run into the sand. In the process, they identified four of the most common leadership development mistakes.

OVERLOOKING CONTEXT

"Context is a critical component of successful leadership. A brilliant leader in one situation does not necessarily perform well in another. There are too many training initiatives that rest on the assumption that one size fits all, and the same group of skills or style of leadership is appropriate regardless of strategy, organizational culture, or CEO mandate.

DECOUPLING REFLECTION FROM REAL WORK

Adults typically retain 10 percent of what they hear in classroom lectures, versus nearly two-thirds by doing. Furthermore, burgeoning leaders, no matter how talented, often struggle to transfer even their most powerful off-site experiences into changed behaviour within the organization.

FAILING TO MEASURE ORGANIZATIONAL RESULTS

We frequently find that companies pay lip service to the importance of developing leadership skills but have no evidence to quantify the value of their investment. Too often, any evaluation of leadership development begins and ends with participant feedback; the danger here is that trainers learn to game the system and deliver a syllabus that is more pleasing than challenging to participants. When businesses fail to track and measure changes in leadership performance over time, they increase the odds that improvement initiatives won't be taken seriously.

UNDERESTIMATING MINDSETS

Becoming a more effective leader often requires changing behaviour. Though most companies who recognize this change are reluctant to address the root causes of why leaders act the way they do."[7]

Most companies recognize a need to adjust underlying mindsets, but they are reluctant to address the root causes of why leaders act the way they do. Just as a coach would view an athlete's muscle pain as a proper response to training, leaders who are stretching themselves should also feel some discomfort as they struggle to reach new levels of leadership performance.

Identifying some of the deepest "below the surface" thoughts, feelings, assumptions, and beliefs is usually a precondition of behavioural change. Promoting the virtues of delegation and empowerment, for example, is fine in theory, but successful adoption is unlikely if the program participants have a clear 'controlling' mindset. It's true that some personality traits (such as extroversion or introversion) are difficult to shift, but people can change the way they see the world and their values. The key message is simple: a cookie-cutter approach will not deliver the desired result without truly understanding context.

The above referenced Mckinsey report provided three examples of context shifts requiring new mindsets. First, the professional-services business wanted senior leaders to initiate more provocative and meaningful discussions with the firm's senior clients. Once the trainers looked below the surface, they discovered that these leaders, though highly successful in their fields, were instinctively uncomfortable and lacking in confidence when conversations moved beyond their narrow functional expertise. As soon as the leaders realized this, and went deeper to understand why, they were able to commit themselves to concrete steps that helped push them to change.

Second, a major European industrial company met strong resistance to their initiative to delegate and decentralize responsibility for capital expenditures and resource allocation to the plant level. Once the issues were put on the table, it became clear that the business-unit leaders were genuinely concerned that the new policy would add to the already severe pressures they faced. They did not trust their subordinates and resented the idea of relinquishing control. Only when they were convinced the new approach would actually save time and serve as a great learning opportunity for more junior managers did the original barriers start to come down. It required a steadfast push from open-minded individuals and mentors to break down the traditional and ineffective model.

Third, a company decided market conditions required its senior sales managers to get smarter about how they identified, valued, and negotiated potential deals. However, sending them on a routine finance course failed to prompt the necessary changes. The sales managers continued to enter into suboptimal and even uneconomic transactions because of a deeply held mindset that their industry was all about market share, that revenue targets had to be met, and that failing to meet those targets would result in losing face. This antiquated mindset shifted when the company set up a process for reflecting on the most critical deals, when peers who got the new message became involved in the coaching, and when the CEO offered direct feedback to participants (including personal calls to sales managers) applauding the new behaviour.

Are the following three mindset traps getting in your way? First, is your organization equipped to deal with your current reality? Second, are you and your organization good at fire fighting and reacting instantly, but not for deciphering the root of your reality? Third, what is the impact of power imbalances and misplaced ego?

COMPETING WILL AND DAMAGING MINDSETS

The following story is a metaphor for competing will and mindsets. One evening, an elder told his grandson about a battle that goes on inside people between two wolves that are inside of us all. One wolf is full of anger, envy, jealousy, sorrow, regret, greed, arrogance, self-pity, guilt, resentment, inferiority, lies, false pride, superiority, and false ego. The other wolf is filled with joy, peace, love, hope, serenity, humility, kindness, benevolence, empathy, generosity, truth, compassion, and faith. The grandson thought about it for a minute, and then asked his grandfather, "Which wolf wins?" The grandfather simply replied, "The one that you feed."[8]

The story serves as an important reminder of the power we have over our experiences and emotions. Often, we look outward to try to make sense of what's going on inside of us. Why? It's our way of coping, and feeling more in control of uncontrollable situations. The problem with this approach, however, is that it takes away our personal responsibility and freedom of choice. In our attempt to feel more in control (by faulting others for our experience) we actually strip ourselves of our own power. As a leader, exercise your freedom of choice and make a decision of which wolf you want to feed. The wolf story is a reminder that our choices have far-reaching effect on our organizations and personal wellbeing. The wolf you choose to feed, will always win.

L. Daskall's leadership blog provides a short summary of damaging leadership behaviour mindsets.

Twelve Dangerous Leadership Mindsets

1. *Seeing the glass as half empty.* Many leaders are guilty of this mindset. Some think that if they point out the bad, that will get people to improve—but we know a negative attitude will never lead to positive results. Nothing will slow your progress like a negative mindset.

2. *Thinking you know people better than you do.* There is a danger in labeling people and putting them into a box when you haven't had a chance to take in their complexity. How can you truly get to know people if your mindset has already told you who they are? Give people a chance to reveal, and sometimes surprise you with, who they really are.

3. *Believing that perfection is a goal.* Perfection doesn't exist and perfect can never be a goal. When you aim to be perfect, you're setting yourself up for failure—either by paralyzing yourself into inaction or by endlessly trying to reach an unreachable goal. Set perfectionism aside and focus on excellence.

4. *Thinking that you never need to rest.* There are leaders who take pride in being constantly on. The reality is, we all need some time off, opportunities to shut down for a while. It is impossible to keep going 24/7 and still be the best you can be. You may think you can do everything and be everywhere, but really you can't. Get some rest.

5. *Assuming that you accomplished great things alone.* Anytime you think you've achieved something by yourself, you're failing to give someone else the credit they deserve. There is no success on a team without the efforts of others, and when you as the leader take all the credit, it costs you respect. Make your language always US and WE, not ME and I.

6. *Not staying present in the moment.* If you're always thinking of where you need to be next instead of staying in the moment, you lose out on precious time and valuable lessons. A constant forward push isn't sustainable in the long term. It burns people out and will lead to low morale and low energy. Give everyone a chance to slow down and experience what's happening now.

7. *Expecting others to do what you're unwilling to do.* How many of us have encountered leaders with a mindset of entitlement? A leader who believes it is about what others can do for them rather than how they can serve others? Entitlement is a dangerous mindset, one that disempowers and alienates people. If you want great people to stick around to serve you, you need to serve them.

8. *Becoming so obsessed with details that you lose the big picture.* There are always details that need legitimate attention, but great leaders know that to get bogged down in all the details and minutia is a waste of time, energy and productivity. Getting stuck in the details will cost you big-picture success.

9. *Isolating yourself from others.* Some leaders actually believe that leadership means immersing yourself in process and procedures instead of being amongst people. The mindset that a leader can't let others too close is one of the most dangerous beliefs. Leadership is all about engagement and empowering others, and you simply cannot do it in isolation. Leaders need people and people need leaders.

10. *Having different sets of rules.* The mindset that you can have one set of rules for yourself and another set for everyone else is disturbing and goes against the principles of service and recognition that leadership should be based on. It leads to disdain and disrespect.

11. *Holding an all-or-nothing orientation.* Failing to recognize nuance and shades of gray leads to bias and distorted thinking. We need leaders who are flexible and agile, unafraid of what might go wrong and positive about what could go right. All or nothing is a dangerous and damaging proposition.

12. *Believing that you have to do everything yourself.* You probably became a leader because you're really good at what you do, but the truth is you never have to do everything alone. Great leaders delegate—which not only helps them but involves other people. If you want things done your own way, teach others how it's done, but bring them in.[9]

Not paying attention to the 12 dangerous mindsets generates a reactive mindset, which propels us to act from human hard drive bias. Paying attention to the dangerous mindsets allows leaders to have different conversations, using a mindfulness mindset. Humanizing leadership helps dampen the reactive mindset of bias.

Are any of the mindsets standing in your way? What are you doing to overcome them? What wolf gets rewarded and fed in your organization? What wolf do you feed?

MINDSET SHIFT

Historically, intelligence has been defined as mental capacity that is fixed, finite, and genetically predetermined. Intelligence has other dimensions as well: physiological and emotional. Daniel Goldman's work on emotional intelligence cites numerous examples that demonstrate how emotional balance and self-awareness are essential components for success in all aspects of our lives. He argues that we must place as much emphasis on emotional skills as we do on intellectual capacities. Standard IQ is rarely an accurate predictor of personal and professional effectiveness.

In the context of organizational transformation, emotional intelligence is the ability to motivate and persist in the face of frustrations—to control impulses and delay gratification, to regulate our mood and keep distress from swamping our ability to think, to empathize, to hope, and to be passionate about our leadership journey.

Axelrod and MacLeod, in *Engaging the Staff,* suggest that to make the people-matter metaphor a reality, we must be inclusive. We must engage people's faculties of reflection, feedback, and decision-making. "We must fight the normal tendency to pull inward. Leadership is about: creating opportunities for people to understand the dangers and opportunities for the organization; fostering broad participation that quickly identifies problems and solutions; sparking innovative and creative thinking and solutions by encouraging different points of view; encouraging collaboration throughout the organization, ensuring that people are connected not only to each other but to the issues as well; and ensuring implementation with accountability by letting people know they have the freedom to carry out the agreed upon plan."[10]

The nature and role of information has to change from being restricted and used for power to being openly shared, to be available to everyone like the air that we breathe. Relationships will flourish when barriers between and among organizational spaces are removed. People will be able to – even compelled – to bump into each other and literally create and circulate new information. As new patterns of interdependence grows, trust will begin to increase due to the recognition that listening skills with a willingness to be influenced become critical. With this, a deep appreciation for diversity of thinking, and inclusion begins to grow.

How to create, support, and maximize mindsets was captured in an essay by MacLeod and Alvarez, "Four Mindset Shifts: Relationships, Identity, Information and People Potential." The four leadership mindset principles articulated below are interconnected. Successful leaders cannot focus on one or two of these principles at the expense of the others. Implementing effective leadership requires the development, practice, and learning of each of these principles so they become self-perpetuating and self-sustaining.

RELATIONSHIP MINDSET

"We don't have to know everything if we trust others. If we are committed to being trustworthy and take personal responsibility to build relationships that model this behaviour, others will deliver the needed results for us.

IDENTITY MINDSET

We understand, and are committed to, what is at stake, and not just for our own end. We must be centered with our organizational vision and surrounded and empowered by a unified and harmonious whole.

INFORMATION MINDSET

We openly share information as a tool for relationship building. Accurate information must be the air that we breathe, and the more open the flow the more easily we can convert data into meaningful knowledge.

COLLECTIVE POTENTIAL MINDSET

We cannot go it alone. To maximize our effectiveness, we must take advantage of the unused skills, talents and potentialities of everyone in the organization, and overcome the intellectual, emotional and systemic barriers that exist. We must create a healthy learning organization."[11]

The Glue

Understanding our human context is a crucial first step to leadership learning. Our personal experience is not what happens to us; what we do externally in relationships is what happens to us. Each of us face countless challenges and choices. Our choices determine the culture of our organizations. We must take time to reflect on our circumstance and ambitions. We need to tap into inspiration and our imagination to create a space where individual and collective relationships flourish. R. Axelrod, in *Terms of Engagement,* asks why old mechanical approaches to change no longer work, and offers to everyone at all organizational levels four principles that shape conversations and help create the glue that bonds the fabric of the human system together.

WIDEN THE CIRCLE OF INVOLVEMENT

"Expand beyond the usual individuals that are typically involved in a change process. In practical terms, widening the circle of involvement means expanding who gets to participate in a change process. We need to engage those we serve, namely our public. It is critical to widen the circle of involvement in order to achieve meaningful and successful outcomes.

CONNECT PEOPLE TO EACH OTHER

Most organizations attempt to connect people through the task at hand. They rely heavily on inspirational talks and slide presentations by leadership and minimize the importance of dialogue. They fail to recognize the significance of relationships! Best practices and their resulting successes stem from meaningful engagement with those who are impacted by the decisions.

CREATE COMMUNITIES FOR ACTION

Community is formed when we create a future together. Employing this principle involves the contribution of all people in the development of procedures and vision. We need to abstain from small-group development strategies, plans, and processes that are presented to the organization as a sales pitch.

PROMOTE FAIRNESS

Democracy is about voice and choice. When we widen the circle of involvement, we hear new voices and perspectives. We must listen deeply and honour the voices we hear. We must promote and exude fairness, information sharing, freedom, and autonomy. When change processes demonstrate these characteristics, the organizational culture shifts from 'You' and 'I' to a collective 'We.' Groups flounder where directionless engagement occurs. Groups are unable to grasp purpose and boundaries while the resulting superficial consensus saps energy and blocks creativity. Their commitment diminishes, leading to mistrust, energy depletion and inconsistent decision-making." [12]

Learning involves taking in new data and applying our experience to transform the data into information. Critical learning can be gained from hypothesizing and abstracting new ways of thinking based on experiences, contemplating what-if scenarios, and considering alternatives. Foresight and wisdom stems from our inner voice and our past understandings.

How are you understanding lessons from the past and realities of the present to see consequences of a decision for the future?

LIBERATION AND AUTHENTICITY

Between Chapter I – What Most Leadership Conversations Gloss Over, and Chapter II – Are Hearts, Spirits and Minds Important to You, fifteen vignettes where presented. This is the eighth and final vignette for Chapter III – Organizational Elasticity and Effectiveness. Collectively the twenty-three vignettes speak to liberation and authenticity in the cultivation of humanizing leadership through reflection, people, and relationships.

Ultimately, leadership influence does not stem from the titles we are given or the marching orders we cast. Influence stems from our liberation— liberation from self-prominence and the trickery of being all-knowing. Influence is earned through the ability to harness the energy and competencies of people. Leadership is about leading, not self-interest. The most profound intellectual and creative concepts will remain dormant without the necessary mechanism to bring the concepts to life. In a human system, that mechanism is the many individuals that participate in the system itself: frontline workers, middle managers, senior managers, board governance, and government.

To test this hypothesis, I asked three senior executives from banking, healthcare, and education sectors, along with a recent PhD graduate, and two emeritus professors who champion leadership development the following question. How important are these leadership tenets; reflection fuels, people matter, and relationships make the difference? I selected response passages that provide a value add to what the book has covered so far.

Kathy Kinlock, President and CEO British Columbia Institute of Technology introduced the analogy of a trapeze bar to describe personal leadership development. "Leaders must first know themselves – and continue to do so over time —to effectively lead and empower others.

The necessity of continuously assessing and re-assessing one's own skills, strengths and challenges over the course of our careers and lives is both an opportunity and a privilege—but not always an easy one. Staring oneself in the mirror, cracks and all, is tough stuff. It's far easier and much more pleasant to shine a light on our existing skills and strengths, but the real learning hides in less illuminated space.

One of my favourite illustrations of this point lies in Danaan Parry's poem "The Trapeze Parable". Parry presents life as a series of trapeze bars that we seize and swing from progressively, grabbing the next bar just after we let go of the previous. Between the bars, in the lesser-known space, is where we experience the most learning. It ends with the beautiful and inspiring sentiment that ...hurtling through the void, we may just learn how to fly. I believe each trapeze bar represents our innate grip on comfort and certainty, and that to learn and advance in our journey we must leap boldly into uncertainty before we can again confidently and comfortably grasp and apply our new skills and knowledge.

The second tenet focuses on teams and people. Exceptional leaders encourage their team members to leap between the bars, take considered risks and achieve new heights. Put simply, we must first ensure we have the right people in the right roles at the right time and then empower them to confidently drive change in themselves and in their functional areas. This happens at a different pace in different organizations.

Thirdly and importantly, I've found that the thread on which all of this hangs is anchored in developing and nurturing a network of people you can trust to tell it like it is, provide unique and valuable insights about the internal and external factors that will impact success, and ensuring you add as much value to this tapestry of connections as you extract. Embrace the personal leadership journey through your own trapeze bars."

Dr. Kevin Smith, President & CEO, University Health Network talks about accomplishments with people is limitless. "As leaders, we have a duty to foster and demonstrate a culture of reflection – which includes examining one's own behaviours, asking tough questions and being unafraid to admit to mistakes or misperceptions. This is especially important in healthcare, where we are entrusted to provide safe, compassionate care to patients and families during some of the most vulnerable moments of their lives.

To support our colleagues, we must equip ourselves with the research; not only of our domain, but also of other domains – like organizational psychology – that conclusively demonstrates that teamwork, respect, diversity and civility are defining characteristics of great places to work. And, to do our best work, we must remember how easy it is to make unproductive decisions by ascribing values to individuals or groups with whom we haven't engaged. What we are able to accomplish when we take the time to build relationships and know people at a human level is limitless."

Mike Bonner, Senior Vice President & Regional Head, BC & Yukon Division, Bank of Montreal introduced time is finite. "People and relationships are key underpinnings for any business or organization's success. As leaders our role is to have the purview and foresight to enable and foster powerful relationships that will be the catalyst to any business. This goes much deeper than a product suite or service offering which are easily copied. I feel the most important aspect of leadership is not telling people what to do rather it is creating and developing powerful relationships that are well understood, committed and trust based. This truly is the secret recipe. In addition to the obvious point of simply having relationships; quality and quantity must also be considered. Time is finite - demands never seem to be - so prioritizing working relationships, where and how you invest your time retaining old ones and developing new ones and juggling authentic relationships that will deliver reciprocal benefits is both essential and healthy.

Lastly, for my personal leadership style, I feel aligning people and their multiple relationships in a common vision helps to rally an organization that is able to maintain culture through people and performance through relationships. Yes, you can have it all."

Harpreet Bassi who reviewed a draft of the book and recently completed a PhD at University of Western Ontario talked about Gen-Xers. "I am struck by a few inter-related thoughts, perhaps overly philosophical. Who decides who is a leader? For many Gen-Xers/emerging leaders such as myself, we see organizational systems producing and identifying leaders based on less than optimal criteria or ideals. Surely we can agree when we look across organizations, leadership characteristics (reflection fuels, people matter, and relationships make the difference) are not common."

Don Philippon, Professor Emeritus University of Alberta covered making mistakes. "Systematic reflection is hard for senior leaders to do both because of their busy schedules but also because leaders do no like to admit weakness. It is through reflection we assess how each of us could improve on our leadership approach. The essence of leadership is to use influence to get things done through people. Influencing others is much easier to do when a relationship of trust exists."

Graham Dickson, Author and Professor Emeritus, Royal Roads University wrapped it all up with a simple ribbon. "Reflection energizes people relationships; healthy people relationships energize organizational results."

To succeed, we will have to first learn who we are. We must determine what we are good at and what we need to learn so we get the full benefit of our strengths. Personal liberation takes time to develop, and is constrained by the shackles we attach to ourselves like our ego, the facade of being all-knowing, the avoidance of our vulnerabilities, ignoring our limitations, and failure to utilize the aid and greatness of those around us. We must lead and inspire by example by personifying the qualities of honesty, integrity, resilience, and confidence, demonstrating how leadership, too, is a process of self-development, not an ultimate arrival. Leadership starts with, and is elevated by, a solid relationship with self. Pretending to know self we walk the fine line of the imposter.

Values manifest through the character ethic of the person and through authentic relationship interaction with others. Being authentic requires being true to one's self and being truthful when dealing with others.

Authenticity dispenses a sense of realness. Integrity is a result of sustaining positive and empathetic relations with others. Trustworthiness is established through our acts of truthfulness and remaining consistent with our voice, behaviour, and actions. Healthy relationships are forged on written and unwritten rules between people. The manner is which we view ourselves will govern and affect how we view others. How we view others will influence how we view ourselves. It is an interactive and interdependent system.

In order to form healthy relationships, it is essential to understand who we are. When we take time to understand ourselves, we can then exhibit deep and genuine empathy and concern for others, and more importantly, speak and act from a place of candidness. If one truly embraces these qualities of character—basic foundational beliefs—then who we are or where we come from does not really matter.

To develop healthy relationships, a certain amount of openness and vulnerability is required. This becomes rather paradoxical for leaders, as we are expected to serve as perfect role models. However, individuals share many of the same hopes, desires, angsts, and apprehensions. In many instances, normal leaders are experiencing the same angst as their team members. Showing vulnerability may create a stronger sense of trust in their relationship with others. Trust is often created when we make ourselves vulnerable to others. Someone must take the first step, and it is recommended that leaders do so, thus demonstrating a willingness to trust others.

Being authentic is being true to one's self and being truthful when dealing with others. It means being steered by purposeful values. Being authentic means being pure, natural, real, and consistent. The leader's role is to enable communication processes and structures that integrate the talents of people and generate creativity and innovation to meet unexpected challenges. A distinguishing feature of the authentic leader's orientation is the exercise of influence, rather than coercive authority, in relation to rules.

A key leadership capability is the capacity to inspire member participation, creativity, and innovation through meaningful engagement toward an inspiring organizational purpose. Innovative and adaptive organizational cultures cannot be 'coerced into place,' an approach that generally produces cultures of fear. They require participation and commitment.

In order to lead without coercion, the authentic leader inspires trust and credibility. The self-reflecting authentic leader understands that organizations are dynamic, living entities constantly evolving in the context of an uncertain, unpredictable environment.

Covey uses the metaphor of the emotional bank account to illustrate the concept of healthy relationships. An emotional bank account, no different than our traditional bank, requires us to make deposits and withdrawals. Covey asserts that we need to make deposits to balance or outweigh the withdrawals we make over time. We build authenticity and trust through positive interactions with others, and in return, this builds the emotional bank account. It is a fragile system that requires a fine balance.

How healthy is your emotional bank account? How are you growing it?

MOVING FORWARD

Some of us, from a very early age, were able to experience value-based relationships where a parent, teacher, or mentor validated us as a person, provided feedback that built us up instead of knocking us down, reduced our fear, and affirmed our importance, presence, and role in the system we were in. They utilized the joy in the value of our contributions, however small, and acknowledged the importance of others and treated them with honour. It was a time of process and valuing.

We have all witnessed difficult interactions that, if tweaked, could have produced a different result. We have all witnessed an episode of sustainable transformation when people truly understood and embraced the organizational vision and its means to achieve its goals. Learning organizations invest in the learning and growth of its people. Building learning organizations requires a basic shift in how we think and interact. Learning gets to the heart of what it means to be human. Through constant learning, we continually re-create ourselves. Through learning, we are able to actualize things we never thought were possible. Through learning, we reinterpret the world and our relationship to it. Through learning, we extend our capacity to create—to be part of the generative process of life.

At its core, an organization is a web of human-system decisions and learning moments bound together through relationships. Human systems are productive, progressive, and healthy when the relationship patterns between its people are sound. Change and proficiency are earned through our ability to harness the energy and competencies of people.

Organizational identity has a profound impact on organizational mindsets and behaviours. Organizational identity is (a) what is taken by employees to be the central attributes of the organization; (b) what makes the organization distinctive, and therefore unique from other organizations in the eyes of the employees; and (c) what is perceived by employees to be enduring or continuing, regardless of objective changes in the organizational environments. The three characteristics described above suggest that organizations with a strong identity have central attributes, are distinctive from other organizations, and remain the same for longer periods. Organizational identity has an impact on organizational proficiency and the attainment of objectives. It provides a way to account for the agency of human action within an organizational framework.

Organizational identity includes three components: feelings of solidarity with the organization; attitudinal and behavioural support for the organization; and the perception of shared characteristics with other organizational members. Organizational identification can affect both the satisfaction and behaviour of employees and the effectiveness of the organization. Before leaders are able to see the future state, they must come to understand organizational values, beliefs, attitudes, and power dynamics. With that understanding comes a sudden awakening of the soft side where culture, purpose, collaboration, and human and relationship capital is valued greatly. With this, the old expression "you cannot see the forest for the trees" takes on a new meaning, as leaders are suddenly able to see the trees, and the spaces between the trees, and the surrounding flora and fauna.

Let's Imagine a Future Where Leaders...

- *Understand* the human context;
- *Operate* from genuine and honourable personal values, principles, and ethics;
- *Shape* and maintain corporate culture;
- *Respond* to, and manage within, dynamic circumstances and contexts;
- *Have* a clear personal purpose and inspire a shared vision with others;
- *Have* healthy relationships that result in integrity of character;
- *Lead* with conviction and courage;
- *Demonstrate* commitment to learning and renewal

REFLECTIONS AND CONSIDERATIONS

What results do you want to create to help people and the organization realize their purpose? What will that future look like, and what will be its vision for achievement? What relationships will need to be built in order to fulfill your vision? Is what you are doing right now helping you get there? What is hampering you in achieving this now? What are you afraid of losing? What might you gain by approaching things differently? How will you work with others to adopt the changes in practice that are necessary?

What is the critical barrier to change and transformation in your organization? Will you discover it before it finds you? How active is the rumour mill in your organization? What issues seem to hinder progress?

If you list the names of people with whom you work most closely, are there relationships you wish to improve or examine?

How are you ensuring everyone shares accountability for achieving the organizational purpose and is imbued with the personal authority to take action?

Are you nurturing a connected human system? Do you overlook information available through your relationships? Do you recognize your responsibility to learn from them?

To what degree do you share what you want and what you feel? When was the last time you examined your attributions and your judgments? When did you last inquire about what someone else wants and feels? How can you alter mindset, communications, and listening skills to generate a different interaction?

If you could, what decisions in the past year would you take back?

Do you agree with this statement? "Any effort to change an organization must begin with you and your specific interactions with specific individuals. A shift from managing others to managing yourself with others." [1]

CHAPTER IV
PARADOX OF SIMULTANEOUS CONTINUITY AND CHANGE

"Stop trying to change reality by attempting
to eliminate complexity."
~David Whyte

INTRODUCTION

Complexity itself cannot be managed. One must be able to perceive, understand, and manage within it; in other words, leaders must engage continually in reflexive and reflective practice living in the present and thinking about the future. This cultivation requires reflection, engaged people, and healthy relationship patterns.

In Chapter IV, I introduce the potential for simultaneous continuity and change of one's personal and organizational identities with their concomitant paradoxical natures that change when one leads in complexity. This leads to a discussion on differentiating complicated and complex scenarios. The art of simplicity meets the puzzle of complexity in two personal stories, which leads to a discussion on complexity leverage and how leaders contribute to complexity. The power of asking questions is examined and the trap of making assumptions is illustrated. I end with a conversation about how far you can see.

SYSTEMIC, PRACTICAL AND PERSONAL CONTRADICTIONS

The business dictionary defines "contradiction" as a combination of statements, conditions, ideas, or features of a situation that is opposed to one another. "Complexity" is defined as a condition having many drivers and autonomous but interrelated and independent components or parts linked through many dense interconnections. In the context of an organization, complexity is associated with interrelationships of individuals, their effect on the organization, and the organization's interrelationships with its external environment. Understanding how these interrelationships arise and how they enable the organization to evolve is crucial. Take a moment and reflect on the contradictions and complexities we have already discussed. Make your list of what stirred you.

The more turbulent the times, and the complexity of the local, provincial, national, and global economy, the more contradictions there are. Yes, we can and should reduce the starkness of some of the contradictions, minimize the inconsistencies, and understand the complexity puzzles. It is impossible to make them disappear, escape from them, or solve them completely, so contradictions and complexity have to be accepted, coped with, and made sense of.

The process of transformation honours the paradox of simultaneous continuity and change. For example, how many of us have survived traumatic events, yet have remained unchanged in our basic values or ideology? We adapt to changing circumstances but tend to remain unchanged at the level of our core beliefs. Others, having endured similar events, become different people in that their basic assumptions have changed considerably. These people are simultaneously the same, yet different. Organizations are no different.

Complexity itself cannot be managed, because it is inherent in all of nature. One must be able to perceive, understand, and manage within; in other words, one must engage continually in reflexive and reflective practice in the living present and thinking about the future.

Meuser and MacLeod, in an essay titled "Lessons from the Stanley Cup Playoffs," say that managing contradictions and complexity requires managing within the paradoxical nature of all interconnection, and participation is a leadership competency requirement. "To suspend the temptation to resolve paradox is difficult for leaders. Many leaders have been schooled in a model of rationality and linear thinking about causality. As we become increasingly aware of all aspects, visible and obscure, of organizational life, comprehending contradictions and complexity can offer some of the most important learning in our lives."[1]

Leadership itself is full of contradictions. What follows are adapted passages from an essay by MacLeod and Dickson titled "Leadership Contradictions" For simplicity, the contradictions have been divided into three categories: systemic contradictions, practical contradictions, and personal contradictions.

Systemic Contradictions

"The dynamics of technology, the rapidity of changes in the external environment, and burgeoning challenges associated with a society of abundance versus scarcity has changed the game of leadership. Social media, just-in-time decision making, the explosion of knowledge and a media dominated public discourse has altered the balance of power between formal leaders, the consumer public, and governments.

Collective decision-making is in a context whereby dialogue and discourse is conducted in an open marketplace and fuelled by ever changing information that is both enhanced and impeded by the same circumstances. Leaders seem to be caught in a tectonic shift, and the distribution of leadership responsibilities between formal and informal leaders. We live in a world where large-scale reform is possible, yet due to the same factors reform remains difficult to achieve. The abundance of the system impels the parts of the system to bolster their independence, while at the same time, the nature of the problems that need to be solved require the exact opposite: interdependence.

Constantly 'shifting sands' of policy environments create a number of contradictions that leaders must deal with. Change itself is the ultimate contradiction, the juxtaposition of our aspirations for the future with our current state. Social media, news media, the internet and technology have sped up the ability to acquaint people with the problems that need fixing and some of the technological solutions have not yet been systematically harnessed by the organizational system to solve them (except in isolated cases).

Another contradiction that emerges in a socio-economic context is created between formal leaders in an organization and the informal consumer leaders. In modern society, the informal leader can marshal knowledge and information and share it like a virus, sometimes creating mass movements, galvanizing public support for specific organizational issues. The authority and resources associated with a formal leader are not constrained by policy and procedure.

Formal leaders may wish to do similar things, but policies, procedures, ethical guidelines and privacy laws that are artifacts from an age when knowledge was scarce hamstring many. They don't have the luxury of singular focus; they need to maintain focus on all aspects of the system on a day-to-day basis and resist being whipsawed by variations of public opinion. Informal leaders are often spurred by passion and common sense; they are not hamstrung in their vision by policy, procedure, rule of law, et cetera. Due to their freedom to act, they can access the media when their case is compelling (and controversial). They also bear no responsibility for overall system performance, advocating solely for their area of personal interest. Contradictions arise when the two remain separate and isolated and do not find ways to work together to create innovation in the system.

A journey of discovery allows one to experience a number of contradictions in, and perspectives of, the organization life realities. Such contradictions influence and re-shape our personal human hard drives and also reformat the hard drives of others. As mentioned earlier, we create, author, edit, produce, direct and act out our own internal drama. For simplicity, we will divide the contradictions or different ways of seeing the world into three categories.

Practical Contradictions

As service delivery entities get larger, senior leaders need to act more strategically, and pay less attention to operational demands, the very demands they excelled prior to being promoted into those senior positions. An additional contradiction is found in the amount of time required to establish large-scale change, the current turnover of leaders and the realities of the existing political process do not stretch across the same time line. It is little wonder why middle-managers committed to an organization or community feel that they can 'wait out' the demands for change that come from the top. We are well aware of our individual accountabilities relative to our designated role, but are we willing to be accountable for our collective results that are a consequence of our ability to work as a member of a team? The tension between collective accountability and individual accountability further illustrates the contradictions we face. And finally, there is the professionalism contradiction: professionals who want to retain their independent professional status, and who have professional organizations to protect it.

Personal Contradictions

Change requires leaders and their followers to change their behaviour. The sheer number of existing contradictions suggest a myriad of behaviour changes for leaders: being better systems thinkers, strategists, communicators, coalition builders, information experts, team-builders, and servant leaders, and the list goes on and on. Each behaviour change is a discrete act of both will and corresponding action.

Behaviour change illuminates the first human contradiction: How do we find the time for reflection and practice in an environment where demands are insatiable and mitigate against these very actions? Given this circumstance, we understand how behavioural change is subject to the amount of change we are able take on.

Leaders find themselves in a place where their intellect prompts them to create significant reform in order to be relevant and master a whole new array of skills to be successful at it. Yet their emotions may tell them to take the time to learn new skills or unlearn behaviours that are no longer desirable. It is no surprise that letting go of what one knows in order to grab onto something new gives leaders pause.

The tension between independence and interdependence, represented by individualistic versus distributed references to leadership, creates further contradiction. Almost by definition, a leader requires a follower, but who is the follower in a distributed leadership approach? Perhaps the term does not apply in this context. Is 'follower' another term for anyone who does not preside over a formal leadership position, or someone who, regardless of role, simply does what he or she is asked to do?

Distributed leadership is a euphemism for sharing the leadership role amongst formal leaders, informal leaders, and consumers that assigns to each a temporary responsibility in the constantly shifting focus of control, depending on the situation and circumstance, and whose influence is required to maintain momentum for change. That said, what does this method look like in practice, and how does it affect learned notions of responsibility and accountability? Will formal leaders 'give up power and control' to informal leaders (e.g., employees and consumers) in the best interests of the change process? Distributed leadership is an admirable concept but a difficult one to operationalize."[2]

Today, leaders must be skilled at being contradictory and paradoxical. Consider this philosophically. Understanding contradictions can be viewed from a traditional Eastern viewpoint or a traditional Western viewpoint. The Western perspective presents contradiction as opposing forces where people move from one behaviour to another depending on a situation, explaining their contradictions in light of situational requirements. The Eastern view adopts the traditional 'Yin-Yang' philosophy, which views a world where 'all universal phenomena are shaped by the integration of two opposite cosmic energies, namely Yin and Yang'. Yin-yang philosophy suggests that, although paradoxes and contradictions are opposing, they are also interdependent and complementary, mutually composing a harmonious whole. In other words, it's okay to appear inconsistent or contradictory.

Do you see a connection between systemic, practical and personal "contradictions" and people matter, and relationships making the difference?

DIFFERENTIATING COMPLICATED AND COMPLEX SCENARIOS

Terms like "complexity, complicated, contradictions and paradoxes," and so on are thrown around loosely in leadership discourse. Each presupposes a parallel between the individual human mind, spirit, heart, and guts and the organizational capability of the collective organizational mind, spirit, heart, and guts to support the planning and execution of new and better solutions to problems and opportunities. Structure, human-resource management, power, culture, strategy, change management, leadership, innovation, knowledge transfer, IT applications, and so on are all interconnecting aspects of connecting people to the organization.

Basically, the organization you work in is a complex system of interacting human elements, roles, responsibilities, and relationships performed by your organizational structures, processes, leadership styles, people's professional and cultural backgrounds, and organizational policies and practices. The level of interconnection of all these aspects will impact the distribution of perception, cognition, emotion, and consciousness within organizations.

Often, we apply simple solutions to complex challenges. We are surprised to only scratch the surface of the challenge at hand. We often fail to understand simple, complicated, and complex problems. With simple problems, the recipe is essential. The recipe is often tested to assure easy replication without the need for any particular expertise. Recipes produce standardized products and the best recipes give good results every time.

A complicated problem requires a formula or elaborate recipe. High levels of expertise, in a variety of fields, are necessary for success. Formulae, or recipes, are critical but not sufficient. High levels of expertise in a variety of fields are necessary for success in dealing with complicated problems.

"A complex problem, such as raising a child, provides experience, but no guarantee of success with the next child. Although experience can contribute to the progress in valuable ways, it provides neither necessary nor sufficient conditions to assure success. Every child is unique and must be understood as an individual. The result is uncertainty of outcome. The complexity of the process and lack of certainty, however, do not lead us to the conclusion that it is impossible to raise a child."[3]

Although experience and expertise can help shape an outcome, it does not provide necessary or sufficient conditions to assure success. Every complex problem is unique and must be understood as such. Even though complex problems present uncertainty of outcome, this does translate to an improbability to solve the issue.

The degree of interconnectedness between the individual parts of a system helps to differentiate complicated and complex scenarios. Challenges that appear to be simple early on may be regarded as complicated when more is known about the challenge. We need to refrain from making assumptions early in the process. We must gain a full understanding of the circumstances and variables at hand before a prognosis is determined.

MacLeod and Cochrane, in an essay titled "Danger of Simplicity," argue that it is time to convert the most critical and complicated questions into complex ones. We need to evolve complicated questions like "What structures do we need to make the organization sustainable?" into a complex question, such as, "How do we build on current structures and relationships to stabilize and enhance organizational outcomes?"[3]

Zimmerman and Globerman, in *Complicated and Complex Systems,* discuss the importance of understanding the difference between complicated and complex systems. They offer three examples.

Three System Definitions

1. *Simple Systems* contain few interactions and are extremely predictable. The same action produces the same result every time. There is a high degree of agreement on outcomes and processes.

2. *Complicated Systems* have many moving parts and many possible interactions but operate in a patterned way. It is possible to make accurate predictions on how a complicated system will behave.

3. *Complex Systems* have characteristics and features that operate in patterned ways, while the interactions within them are continually changing. With complex systems, there is a low level of agreement on the outcomes or processes. Situations involve multiple individuals or processes and there is a high degree of heterogeneity among them. In addition, teams may self-organize around areas of competence, making relationships and resulting interactions even more fluid. [4]

Courage and conviction are essential traits for coping with the ambiguities associated with constant complex challenges. Courageous leaders share a number of key characteristics: insight, initiative, influence, impact, and integrity. They are able to look at complex situations, gain clarity, and determine a course of action. They do not sit on the sidelines waiting for a change in circumstance. They do not ask others to do what they are unwilling to do themselves, and they lead by example.

How are you developing your skill to reframe and convert complicated and complex questions?

EXPERIENCING COMPLEXITY
FIRST HAND

My time as lead of the Government of Ontario Climate Change Secretariat expanded my thinking about inter-relationships and contradictions between complex systems. Each and every week I witnessed separate conversations about climate change, economy, and health. Convention dictated that there is something called healthcare, something called environmental protection and something else again called the economy. Yes, they look at different issues, use different language and depend on different types of expertise. Yet, I was beginning to see how they were connected and was also beginning to see that we will never fully optimize progress in any of these domains unless we begin to think of them holistically. What follows are adaptations from an essay I wrote titled "How We Live, Where We Live, How We Make A Living."

"How we live, where we live and how we make our living are so tightly integrated that it is impossible to think of one without the other two. If we think of healthcare in isolation, we can easily focus on curing people of disease. Yet a reduction in infant mortality is of limited value if it means more children survive disease to die of poverty and starvation. If we think of the environment in isolation we can expend huge efforts to preserve the wilderness yet remain heedless of the human destitution just outside the borders of wildlife sanctuaries. If we think of the economy in isolation, we will focus on growth as the only measure of human development but ignore its effects on resource depletion, pollution, an overindulgent lifestyle and even mental stress.

Science has shown us again and again that our reality consists of ecologies, systems, and networks, yet our preference for compartmentalized thinking persists in breaking problems down in ways that refuse to see larger interrelationships. Looking only at the domains that we've arranged neatly in silos, we fall victim to the law of unintended consequences. We pull economic levers and are surprised by their unexpected effects on health or the environment. We pull healthcare levers and are shocked to find spiraling costs the economy simply cannot sustain

The global economic situation we find ourselves in today has shown us the extent to which we live in a highly interdependent global world where boundaries matter less than the urgency with which we can devise transnational solutions like free trade agreements.

Our real difficulty lies in how we frame the problem and our inability to think about complex challenges holistically. Nowhere are the effects of compartmentalization more harmful than in the economic concept of externalities. These are the items that are "off the books" and never factored into the complete costs of any economic activity. A company dumping industrial waste into a river considers its clean up as an "externality" that does not figure into its cost calculations. It is someone else's problem. A computer manufacturer prices its products without worrying about the time and effort that will be needed to dispose of components, some of which are health threats, once the products become obsolete. Just think about the amount of industrial waste we send offshore to be out of sight and mind."[5]

We have compartmentalized our thinking about the economy so as to ignore its effects on health or the environment. The World Health Organization has identified climate change as one of the top three current threats to human health. Today we recognize as never before the impact of environmental degradation on human health: the ozone layer and skin cancers, mercury in seafood and neurological diseases, air pollution and respiratory diseases, wastewater contamination and outbreaks of e-coli – the list goes on and on. A potential proliferation of these health challenges could have a crippling effect on business and our economy in terms of rising absenteeism, high turnover, and low productivity.

Let's take health and the environment, not only do they share common interests – they share common solution sets. Both are technology intensive and do not look for a single technological fix. Both have learned to emphasize prevention instead of remediation as the most cost-effective way to achieve their objectives. And both recognize the critical importance of attitudinal changes in mindsets, behaviours and leadership.

Given these commonalities, it seems intuitively obvious that the lessons learned in one area can inform understanding and accelerate progress in the other. Since people have been concerned about their health for much longer than they have been aware of environmental degradation there is much that environmentalists can learn from health care workers about changing attitudes and promoting new mind-sets.

Consider that half a century ago smoking was ubiquitous in society: today it is visible only among a dwindling minority huddled around building entrances. Progress is also being made in public campaigns to promote fitness and healthier diets. We may not yet be as healthy as we would like, but at least we can see the importance of public awareness campaigns in moving toward preventing avoidable illness. All of this suggests that there are synergistic gains to be made from more closely associating and aligning the efforts of the health care community with those dedicated to environmental issues.

The challenge is how to benefit from a systems approach without it becoming disempowering. At a certain point, problems can seem too vast and complex to design holistic interventions. With climate change, economy, and health, we have people and politicians feeling overwhelmed by the complexity and the reality that it touches on so many different parts of our lives. Mobilizing support for discrete quick fix actions is often more expedient than broader comprehensive approaches. We are a society that loves piecemeal approaches in many respects.

Outgrowing today's challenges with a stronger picture (reflection fuels) will not be characterized by a magic bullet or a single technology. The picture will be framed by broadly based initiatives that secure participation from the grassroots (people). The picture will embody a holistic approach (new relationship building) that breaks down silos, aligns motivations, and associates incentives. The picture will consist of thousands of small steps all leading in the same direction.

How are you reshaping your thinking to benefit from a broader perspective while still moving forward and taking action?

COMPLEXITY TO THE RESCUE

Ron Short suggests we all participate in multiple systems many times a day. "Each occasion requires appropriate, here and now structures to achieve objectives. Every relationship constitutes as different system. Add someone to a relationship, and you have another system. Add more, and it is yet another system. Then, (this is critical information) your system not only changes with different people, it changes when the same people converse about different topic."[6]

For instance, you have a colleague who is also a friend. That is one system. However, when the two of you talk about business, you are immediately in different roles, which is another system. When you and your colleagues discuss markets, return of investment, budget this is another system. When you brainstorm ideas, that is yet another. They all bring different roles and different systems.

P. Plsek in the article, "Redesigning Healthcare With Insights From The Science Of Complex Adaptive Systems", suggests: "As a leader think of yourself as flipping and flopping in and out of systems from moment to moment. Each time your system changes with people or different topics, the structure of roles, as well as learning patterns, also change."[7]

Most complex adaptive systems are in a constant state of change and respond to external environment changes. This happens whether we acknowledge it or not. Complexity looks at interacting elements and asks how they form patterns and how those patterns unfold. This kind of inquiry can create mixed reactions. Lindstrom and MacLeod, in an essay titled "Getting a Grip on Complexity," suggest "traditional science does not like any perpetual novelty. Newtonian laws are supposed to be unchanging. Far too often we apply simple solutions to complex challenges and then become bewildered as to why we have only scratched the surface of our issues."[8]

It is not an easy task, as Plsek explains: "One of the hallmarks of wisdom, that distinguishes it so sharply from 'mere' intelligence, is the ability to exercise good judgment in the face of imperfect knowledge."[7] From a leader's perspective, imperfect knowledge abounds in complex organizational systems, yet good judgment and decision-making are necessarily expected of them, if not taken for granted. Many organizational systems are more than just complex; they are also complex adaptive systems (CASs). The latter is distinguished by characteristics including elements that can adapt or change; a few simple rules of behaviour; nonlinear relationships; emergent behaviour; unpredictability; self-organization; contextual dependency; and healthy tensions.

We must enter a new kind of leadership that understands and embraces complexity. Marion and Uhl-Bien, in *Leadership in Complex Organizations*, put it this way: "Leaders understand that the best innovations, structures, and solutions to problems are not necessarily those that they, with their limited wisdom, ordain, but those that emerge when interacting aggregates linkages in a system that evolve from individual interactions work through issues."[9]

In spite of the tremendous insights the theory and work of natural systems can teach us about social constructs in organizations, we often fail to learn from nature's lessons. In terms of complexity and change, Capra has written persuasively about this seeming paradox: continuous change, adaptation, and creativity. Yet our business organizations seem to be incapable of dealing with change. Capra, in *Hidden Connections*, proposes a holistic alternative to linear and reductionist theory: "Understanding human organizations as living systems is one of the critical challenges of our time."[10]

So, what does all this mean in the context of a leader's challenge?

First, getting back to Capra's key insight, organizational systems need to be understood and respected as a living system with all its characteristics at play, not merely as a nice metaphor. Only then may we be able to speak the same language and move forward on some common ground.

Second, we need to respect complexity and figure out what we can and cannot do. Flood talks about getting to grips with complexity. This is where the practice of wise leadership is critical. The further away in space and time we venture from our locality, the more mythical our interpretation of things, such as simple and complex, become.

Third, we need to seek and apply the available researched evidence on leadership and change management. While this seems trite to suggest, it is clear this does not regularly happen. Where is the accountability for not practicing evidence-informed policy and decision-making in governance, leadership, and management at all levels? Integrating research evidence into policy and decision-making practice remains stubbornly sporadic and limited despite the rhetoric. To still view these as "separate" activities is foolish, if not hypocritical. Part of the issue stems from prevailing mindsets and confusion about what research is, or is not, particularly when entering the world of qualitative inquiry and collaborative, action-oriented research. Will have more discussion on this in Chapter V.

Are you stopping to extract simple nuances from complex problems or are you stopping to understand complexity?

LEADERS CONTRIBUTE
TO COMPLEXITY

Complexity is found in daily social interaction. Leaders, like all others within the organization, contribute to its complexity. Whether an issue is thought to be simple or complicated, complexity is ever-present. It cannot be managed out of a situation; wherever human beings gather, complexity lives. No person can decide or intend for another; outcomes cannot be predicted or controlled. The source for uncertainty lies within the individual and group who, paradoxically, are indivisible. It is impossible to make accurate predictions of how a complicated system will behave.

We can work to simplify processes and recognize patterns, but we must be aware that patterns do not necessarily repeat in the exact same way. The paradox of continuity and change is continually operative. Crisis and opportunity are inseparable. In a crisis, there is an opportunity for change but not a guarantee. In opportunity, there is a possibility for stasis or change but no guarantee for one or the other. Herein resides the difference between change, which is adaptive, and transformation, which involves a shift from one form to another.

Understanding the paradoxical nature of organizations prepares leaders to handle complicated processes. Understanding that organizational problems are simple and complicated at the same time helps to avoid cookie-cutter approaches. Processes are paradoxically linear and dynamic, thus requiring knowledge about, and intervention in, both spheres. Treating paradox as polarity means that attention is often placed on one pole at the expense of the other. To devise interventions based on one pole in the absence of the other will lead to unexpected consequences. Belief that one's genetic makeup is somehow removed from environmental conditions leads us to believe that we can remove the individual from his or her environment. We need to understand that simple and complicated are paradoxical in nature, and that complexity and complexity thinking are different. Each of represents a non-linear, dynamic dimension of reality that requires an informed and mindful understanding.

As we will discuss in more detail in Chapter V, most complex and adaptive organizational systems are constantly adapting and changing as external environments change. This is happening whether or not we understand or attempt to understand and influence the process that led to the emergence of new patterns and relationships within complex adaptive systems. In *The Fifth Discipline: The Art and Practice of the Learning Organization*, Peter Senge suggests eleven laws of systems thinking that help us understand systems and complexity better.

Eleven Laws of System Thinking

1. *Today's problems come from yesterday's solutions.* Leaders are happy to solve problems, but don't always think about intended and unintended consequences. Too often our solutions strike back to create new problems.

2. *The harder you push, the harder the system pushes back.* Humans have a stubborn tendency to bully our way through tough situations when things are not working out as we would hope. We charge ahead without taking time to think through solutions to find better alternatives. Sometimes we solve problems; more often, especially in the current environment, we find ourselves up to our ears in more problems.

3. *Behaviour grows better before it grows worse.* Short-term solutions give temporary improvement at best but never eliminate fundamental issues and problems. These underlying problems will make the situation worse in the long run.

---

4. *The easy way out leads back in.* Leaders often have a few quick fixes in their 'quiver' of solutions that have brought quick and easy success in the past. Too often, the easy way out is retrofitting these fixes to any situation without regard to the unique contexts, people and timing.

5. *The cure can be worse than the disease.* Often, the easy and familiar solution is not only ineffective but addictive and dangerous. It might even induce dependency.

6. *Faster is slower.* At the first taste of success, it is tempting to advance at full speed without caution. Remember that the optimal rate of growth or change is far slower than the fastest growth or change that is possible.

7. *Cause and effect are not always closely related in time and space.* We are good at finding causes, even if they are just symptoms unrelated to root causes.

8. *Small changes can produce big results—but the areas of highest leverage are often the least obvious.* The most grand and splashy solutions—like changing organization policy, vision, branding or tagline—seldom work for transforming change. Small, ordinary but consistent and repetitive changes can make a huge difference.

9. *You can have your cake and eat it too—but not all at once.* Rigid 'either/or' choices are not uncommon. Remember that this is not a dilemma if we change our perspective or the 'rules' of the system.

10. *Dividing an elephant in half does not produce two small elephants.* As a leader, you can fail to see the system as a whole at your peril. This flaw in perception and vision often leads to suboptimal decisions, repeated tasks, lost time and energy, and maybe even losing followers.

11. *There is no blame.* People and organizations like to blame, point fingers and raise suspicions about events, situations, problems, errors and mistakes. Sometimes we even believe the blame we throw around. In reality, we and the cause of events, situations, problems, errors and mistakes are part of the system.[11]

The 'Laws" offer an insight into new mental models, new ways of perceiving and understanding the effects of interventions in a dynamic human system like an organization. The laws show that all our solutions have consequences, sometimes bad and unexpected. The laws call us to understand relationships, and cause and effect chains. The laws ask us to perceive systems as a whole and as a part of other systems. Yes, there are many challenges to system thinking. Many we can defeat with gaining and using knowledge how systems work. The most serious challenge is our own human nature. Our passions, emotions and instincts can easily defy the rational and systematic way of thinking. What's your reaction to this: First step to master the system thinking is to learn how to cooperate with yourself.

By paying attention to the laws, I found myself: thinking more about what really might be at the root of a performance problem before identifying a solution; looking for root causes in the processes and systems instead of people; turning to data or other measures to help identify underlying systemic patterns or dynamics; exploring the likely unintended consequences of potential solutions before choosing one; reflecting on my past experiences to avoid repeating mistakes; carefully considering the options for implementation of a solutions before fully committing to them; embedding one improvement at a time, rather than trading off seemingly conflicting goals; and being more patient and objective in making final decisions.

Can you think of examples in your experiences where these laws have played out?

ASKING THE UNASKABLE AND THINKING THE UNTHINKABLE

Gandhi said, "We stand within a circle whose circumference is bounded by our fears. The circle is our comfort zone; if we stay there, we become complacent."[12] For the most part, whenever people get together to have an organizational conversion two conversations take place—what people are saying publicly and the private unfolding in our head. Often the discourse consists of polite banter or debate that falls short of naming the big elephants standing in the way of progress. L. Ledoux suggests,"the capacity for naming elephants in the room, tough issues that no one talks about, is a common defining characteristic and behaviour in an organization with extraordinary adaptability."[13] These organizations have moved the water cooler, cafeteria, and behind-the-back lamentations to the front.

We need to bring to the surface the fundamental issues that suppress our ability to spring forward and bring about improvement. We must tackle the paradox or tension in the implicit assumptions we hold. Scharmer and Kaufer in *"Leading from the Emerging Future"* describe three "openings" needed to transform organizations: opening the mind (to challenge our assumptions), opening the heart (to be vulnerable and to truly hear one another), and opening the will (to let go of pre-set goals and agendas and see what is really needed and possible). "These three openings match the mindset blind spots of most change efforts, which are often based on rigid assumptions and agendas. Well-intentioned change efforts will collapse if leaders are unable or unwilling to embrace this simple truth."[14]

Letting go of control creates the space for relationships and a collective identity to develop, for information to be shared, and for the talents of everyone within the system to be valued and used. On the strength of these behavioural and mindset shifts, we can achieve the collective accountability required for making significant organizational improvements. We can become much more adept at examining our emotional triggers, thinking patterns, assumptions, values, principles, strengths, and limitations.

Some leaders consider historical outcomes when making their decisions. They think about how things were. They ask, "What happened? What went wrong? How can we protect gains?" These leaders require certainty in order to try new things. They admire people who don't make waves. Stability and systems are the benefits past-thinking leaders bring to organizations.

Some leaders focus on the present when making decisions. They're practical thinkers. The Educause blog article titled "Asking Questions Can Help You Become a Better Leader" suggests "present-thinking leaders live in the moment. They ask, what's happening now? What needs to be done? What resources do we currently have? These leaders neglect the future because of present responsibility. They admire discipline in others and judge people by how well they complete tasks. Present thinking leaders bring consistency and reliability to their organizations."[15]

Some leaders look into the future when choosing what to do. They love new ideas and creative thinking. They ponder what could be and who people might become. They continually ask why and why not.

If we fail to explore our assumptions, we will continue to be held hostage by exhausted and obsolete mindsets and activity. We cannot afford to stick to the same old mental models that fail us repeatedly. We must let go of the "fixes that fail." Any improvement potential remains inert unless we acquire new ways of seeing and understanding. The conclusions we draw and the beliefs we adopt are based off our assumptions. Inconsistencies can arise in our assumptions, and in turn hold us back from achieving our purpose. Continual investigation of our assumptions is paramount; we must purge our blockages and refine our vision so we can develop genuine solutions to organizational challenges. That said, it is not easy or comfortable to expose our held assumptions. We have applied these assumptions and inserted them deep within our foundation. These assumptions have helped form our previous policies and actions. To depart from these assumptions now requires an acceptance of their expiration or futility. When we explore assumptions in collaboration with others, we are provided an opportunity to detect patterns and the differences in our collective thought. These patterns and differences can establish common ground and produce creative alternatives for stubborn problems.

Asking "why" questions guides us to do and say the right things. By engaging people in dialogue, wicked questions invite exploration into inconsistencies in thought that have held us back from achieving our purpose and can be used to promote a search for local solutions to organizational challenges. Asking "why" questions of self and others break the ritual conversations that take place.

Do you ask this key "why" question? Why have I tolerated behaviour in myself and in others that conflict with a commitment to the purpose and vision of my organization?

What's your skill level in the framing of the question, the timing of the asking, in a manner that creates commitment to continuously learn? The listening side of the question asked is listening to hear, to understand, versus listening to counter.

HOW WELL DO YOU ASK

Would you agree that most organizational conversations skirt over radical ideas and painful interpretations of conflicting perspectives? Do you see most discourse consisting primarily of polite banter or debate that falls short of naming conflict? What is your contribution?

The Educuase blog asks, "How well do you ask questions? The 'ability to ask questions' doesn't usually show up on any list of leadership competencies or job-description requirements. However, asking effective questions is a major component of any leader's job, and asking the proper questions often distinguishes outstanding leaders from average ones (or worse, poor ones). Here's why asking questions is important: It helps you uncover the challenges you're facing and generates better solutions to solve those problems. Too much time and energy is spent solving the first iteration of a challenge with the first idea we have. This approach is both limiting and counterproductive. The right question can create remarkable moments and can progress into innovation and growth. It keeps us in learning mode rather than judgment mode. If we're asking a question, we're not rushing in to provide the answer, give the solution, or take on the challenge. "[15]

Asking questions is a proficient self-management tool to keep us focused on the bigger picture, and as a leader, that's our responsibility to our team and to the organization. My appointment to lead a very large and complex organization put the hypothesis to the test. Every day I entered my new office with a combination of excitement and anxiousness in my belly. Daily, I lived on a three-dimensional chessboard with new players, agendas, and polarity. I encountered moments of self-doubt and moments of panic.

Over the years, I had surrounded myself with leadership manuals, books, and articles. I had memorized the leadership and change-management frameworks. I played with the models and archetypes, trying to absorb as much as I could, but I realized they were not going to give me what I needed as a leader. The more I listened, the better my questions became and the more I learned. Questions also helped me clarify my own thinking on projects, workflow, and strategies for my new role. In the process, my delegation skills reached a new level. I asked myself why it was easier to delegate in this new complex and unfamiliar world versus my familiar old world. What did I learn? I realized that I liked to hold on to things.

Leaders who do all the talking are tone deaf to the needs of others. Unfortunately, some of these types of leaders feel that being the first and last person to speak is a sign of strength. In reality, it's the exact opposite. Such an approach cuts information off at its source, from the very people— staff, colleagues, and customers—you should trust the most. Being curious is essential to asking good questions. We need to stay curious longer, and at times offer advice at a slower pace. Getting to a solution quickly is not always the best route to take. This is easy to say and hard to do, but with practice we can all improve this skill.

Leaders should ask questions that get people to describe what happened and what they were thinking. Open-ended questions prevent us from making judgments based on assumptions and can elicit some unexpected answers that can lead to better results. Constructing questions that use "what," "how," and "why" encourages dialogue. Keeping the conversation open and flowing is critical to finding better solutions. It also makes us better leaders and managers.

When we ask meaningful questions, it shows that we care. Especially when our meaningful questions are paired with positive and authentic facial expressions and engaged body language. This combination furthers conversation and encourages the person to share information that could be important. For example, if we are interviewing a job candidate, we don't only want to encourage them to talk about their accomplishments and their setbacks and how they dealt with them. An interested interviewer can often get someone to talk in depth about rebounding from failure. However, people will only open up if we actively show interest and listen attentively.

Too often leaders make the mistake of assuming everything is going okay when there is an absence of negative news. This is a colossal mistake. The lack of negative news can suggest people are afraid to share anything but good news, even if it means stonewalling. When information surfaces during our conversations and meetings, we need to dig for details without blaming. We need to focus on learning rather than judging and ask the questions that will help expose the entire picture. Remember, problems within our teams are, first and foremost, our problems.

"Asking good questions, and doing so in a spirit of honest information gathering and collaboration, is good practice for leaders. It cultivates an environment where staff feels comfortable discussing issues that affect both their performance and that of the team. This in turn, creates a foundation for deeper levels of trust, increased morale and innovation, and enhanced productivity."[15]

Probing questioning, including questions about existing authority and cartel structures, contain the answers we require to resolve today's challenges. The freedom to ask questions from an honest space enables us to outgrow our current constraints. It is crucial to test held assumptions by asking precise and complete question. The presenting problems we face are rarely the actual problems. We need to be more forthright and transparent in our dialogue, and unafraid to confront some harsh truths. The language of concealment and a too-genteel discourse create complacency and dull the perception of our joint shortcomings.

At times, we remain quiet when we should be asking questions. We keep talking when we should be listening. Worst of all, we fail to acknowledge what is right in front of our noses, and we miss out on the opportunities before us.

How tolerant are you of silence? How much silence can you stand before you feel compelled to say something? "Silence has a purpose, and it gives people time to absorb what you have said. It contains content; tension, relief, peace, or curiosity."[13]

WHEN ASSUMPTIONS TROUNCE TRUTH

Working in a hospital Intensive Care Unit (ICU) is an experience that is difficult to put into words. It is an intense and frenzy-paced environment, where the provider stress levels can mirror that of the trauma patients in some situations. In an essay by Gowen and MacLeod titled "Caring, Coping, Crying," we capture through a story line personal work experiences, and assumptions made. The setting for the story is a hospital intensive care unit. The message on making assumptions can apply to all work environments.

"I can promise you that you do not want to be a patient in my unit. If you are, then that means you're really sick. If you end up here I can promise you will get stellar care from the best available team of health care providers. Often at times we may act a little wacky, though. We may seem rude at other times. Maybe you catch us acting totally inappropriate in relation to the situation at hand. Maybe you have even thought, 'How can they act this way with the condition my family member is in?'

You walked in to me singing a song out loud as I hung that IV medicine, huh? You were a little bewildered, and thought, 'is that from *The Sound of Music?* Why is she so inappropriately jolly considering my dad has a tube down his throat?' I'm not singing for my own satisfaction. What you don't realize is I'm singing to calm my nerves, to keep myself relaxed. Your dad almost died before I let you back in. I'm concerned for him, but I don't want you to see that on my face. I don't want you to worry about him. That's my job. I just want you to love him.

I know you just heard us laughing and cracking a joke in the hall. I get it. You don't see anything funny with your mom confined to that bed, attached to all those monitors. I understand. I do. Please understand that while you were waiting outside we saved the young woman next door. She couldn't breathe. Now she can. We didn't think we'd get a breathing tube down in time. We also restarted the heart of the man across the hall. We were unsure if his heart would restart, but it did. The patient next door to him wasn't so lucky. We tried. I begged God, but she went anyway. I held her daughter and let her cry in my hair for twenty minutes.

Sometimes we have to laugh. It's the only thing we know to do in these moments. If we cry, we are afraid we won't be able to stop. I'm really sorry if I seemed short with you when you came in to visit. I know you thought I was being rude. I know you complained about me, saying, 'She must have wanted a break instead of taking the time to talk to me!' No. I won't get a break today; once again, we are short-staffed. I wasn't trying to be rude. I was focused on the change I just noticed on your dad's EKG. I was trying to figure out what I could try next when his blood pressure plummets again. You see, I'm giving the maximum amount of all those drugs you see hanging. I know you're not ready to say goodbye. I'm not ready to give up. That distracts me at times and impacts my ability to converse.

I want you to know that when I see your mom in this condition I feel your pain. I think of my own mom who has passed away. When their conditions mirror each other, so similar in presentation, it's feels like peeling the scab off my grief. I don't let you see that, but I choke back my own tears while you cry.

Oh, dear mom, as you try to maintain your composure while your child remains unresponsive, I have to fight to keep from sobbing all over your shirt while I hug you. Your plight is a very real confrontation of the frailty of our children. I don't like it as a mother. I will sweat blood to fight for your baby's life, no matter the age. I know it could be mine just as easily.

My dear sir, as you cry over your ailing spouse, I'm sorry that I have to walk away. I'm sorry I can't be stronger for you. For a moment, I place myself in your shoes. I imagine my spouse lying there, and I grieve with you. Then I get back on the horse and I fight for your bride. I just wanted you to know that.

My singing, dancing, laughing behaviour might make you think I'm indifferent. Or my distraction and firmly set expression might make you think I don't care. But I do. What you don't see is when I pull into my driveway at the end of my long shift. Often times, I put my car into park and I cry. All the stress of fighting for them, all the grief pushed away, all the emotions finally have time to catch up with me. I don't sing or laugh. I weep. Then I wipe my eyes and go inside. I hug my babies a little tighter. I hold my spouse as little closer. Then I go to bed early so I can come back in the morning to care, to listen and to ask."[16]

Think about a recent event/meeting you were in. Did your personal assumptions accurately reflect the current realities?

HOW FAR CAN YOU SEE

Our world is often described as volatile, uncertain, complex, and ambiguous, with major tectonic shifts that demand a new adaptive mindset of leadership. Every month, we hear about the disruption of market leaders. Think about all the big retail chains that have closed. The average lifespan of an S&P 500 company has gone from sixty-seven years in 1937 to seventeen years in 2016. Think about Sears, Lehman Brothers, Dell Computers, Avon Products, Radio Shack—the list goes on and on. With advances in technology, mobiles are becoming more of a convergence device that replaces so many utilities (calculators, alarm clocks, small digital cameras etc.) that we used otherwise. Workplaces are changing, and every new generation brings different values, expectations, and mindsets to work. A rise in automation is creating heavy disruption. From how products are purchased to booking taxies and filing tax returns, everything is increasingly being automated. The agents, middlemen, and the whole supply chain related to these services have been disrupted. Wait until automated cars become the next big frontier for the technology battle.

As we move into the high-velocity context of the 21st-century economy, leaders will need to be open to a future not yet created. In that sense, our own future is a blank canvas. Leverage lies in understanding dynamic complexity and seeing inter-relationships rather than linear cause-and-effect chains. Leaders must master an ability to remain relevant in today's fast-paced and exponentially changing world. Swimme and Tucker remind us that the nature of the universe is to move forward amongst great tensions between dynamic and opposing forces. If creative energies, in the heart of the universe, have succeeded so brilliantly in the past, we have reason to hope that such creativity will inspire and guide us into the future.

In the future, everything is portable. Location doesn't matter, presence does. Connections with customers are dynamic. Apps will allow individuals to take charge of many aspects of their life that previously required a series of personal interventions by others. Just look at how consumer preferences, big data, and personal technology have revolutionized the media, entertainment, and retail sectors. Think about the following examples of major customer transformations from social media, retail, and taxi and accommodation services. UBER—the world's largest taxi company—owns no vehicles. FACEBOOK—the world's most popular media owner—creates no content, ALIBABA—the world's most valuable retailer—has no inventory. AIRBNB—the world's largest accommodation provider—owns no real estate.

A common thread is technology as an enabler to create relationships with a diverse population and make it easy for people to enable customization of service. In the new digital, personalized, portable, global world, power shifts to the consumer.

With a hyper-connected workforce, organization cultures have become transparent. With opportunities abounding, employees are "volunteers" who have global choices. In this world, having a compelling purpose is a mandatory prerequisite for profits to follow. "Traditional hierarchical structures are fading away to give way to purposeful networks and communities of people working together to achieve a shared purpose. The cumulative impact of these forces demands a new mindset and competences for leaders to be able to stay relevant and make a positive difference to people and hence, business." [17]

The speed of change is no longer linear; it is exponential. The very fabric of organizations is on the cusp of being changed by technology in remarkable ways. Robots are now performing routine tasks. Artificial Intelligence (AI) is beginning to outperform human beings in trials. These new discoveries and inventions will become the instant rock stars of the business world, able to swiftly analyze vast amounts of information from a population to make very specific and highly informed decisions for individuals.

Revell, in a *New Science Magazine* article titled "Google Deep Mind NHS Data," suggests that technology giants "such as Google and Apple have entered the healthcare arena. Earlier this year, *New Scientist Magazine* reported that Google's Deep Mind AI system has been given access to data on 1.6 million patients in the UK. The Japanese government has challenged technology companies to develop $1000 robots to assist healthcare workers in basic tasks such as lifting patients. The future has arrived and it looks much different than the past."[18]

With global databases, clouds, and supercomputer analytics at hand, people have access to information that has a profound effect on how they chose to engage with the formal healthcare system. Personalized medicine is the next frontier. It is already allowing us to customize treatments and therapies to highly specialized individual needs. Our DNA is our personal data centre, and it will be the patients' choice as to who has access to their personal health information.

We must open up our organizational systems so we can adapt to these changes and others. To do this, we need a remarkable change, and the willingness to let go of historic structures and practices, so that we can embrace fundamentally new models, fuelled by those we serve and the newest technologies.

Today, we have an opportunity to stamp out cynicism by building trust, energy, and respect among the many diverse players in this ecosystem. This means coming to the table as a partner, an enabler, and a learner. Changing mindsets, including our own, is about more than changing minds. It requires bold and truthful conversations among equals. It means leaving our egos at the door and taking risks. Coming together will unleash new ideas, generate new conversations, and foster a new energy around change. Imagine the power of previously fragmented and silenced voices joining together to shape a future rather than being asked to merely sanction it.

Posner and Kouzes, in *The Truth About Leadership,* came to the following conclusion after surveying thousands of people on ideal leadership qualities: "The ability to look forward is second only to honesty as the most admired leadership trait. Focusing on the future sets leaders apart. While leadership has evolved over time, the following five areas of focus have remained constant as the key functions of effective leaders across all industries: strategist—shaping the future; executor—making things happen; talent manager—engaging today's workers; human capital developer—building the next generation; personal proficiency—investing in their own development. These five areas of focus help organizations answer the question "where are we going?[19]

Here's the problem: In tough economic times, everyone hunkers down on tactics. They focus on survival and results. Decisions become pragmatic. After a while, however, this short-term approach grinds us down, and we lose sight of the big picture. In today's difficult times, people need to be reminded of why they are doing what they do, and why it matters. This is when leaders can step up and make a difference. Leadership is more than encouraging high-performance; it's about reminding people of what they are trying to build and why it matters. In many ways, leadership supplies oxygen to keep the fires going. When people are mired in day-to-day work details, they can lose their bearings.

Posner and Kouzes go on to suggest three ways to expand your ability to become more future oriented and improve your leadership effectiveness.

INSIGHT

"Looking for repeating themes and messages in our lives that remind us of what matters most. For younger leaders, there's less past to recall; however, it's still important to use the richness of our life experiences to uncover ideals.

OUTSIGHT

To be a credible leader, we need to spend more time reading, thinking, and talking about long-term possibilities. We need to improve our understanding of the world around us, not just in our industry. A game-changing product in an unrelated field could impact our customers and their need for our services.

FORESIGHT

There is a dramatic difference between people who react to roadblocks with a sense of futility and pessimism and those who react with determination and optimism. Those who learn to be optimistic about life and work are far more likely to be successful than those who view a current event through the pessimist's lens. Being optimistic doesn't mean ignoring reality or the hardships required to get great results" [19]

The more you understand reality, the more prepared you are to endure hardships and adversity. Optimism, and a vision for what's possible, supplies the energy to keep going, persist through challenges, and come out on the other side. D. Pollard in his blog post "System Thinking and Complexity 101" introduced a model for identifying and dealing with reality in both the complicated and complex aspects of issues we face in our own lives, and in our organizations.

System Thinking and Complexity		
COMPLICATED PROBLEM	*IMAGINE*	COMPLEX PREDICAMENT
Analyze	*QUESTION*	Explore
Deduce	*CONVERSE*	Intuit
Intervene	*COLLABORATE*	Adapt & Workaround

The model presents an elementary method of thinking about insight, outright and foresight in both complicated and complex situations as a means of better understanding and appreciating them. Pollard suggests: "This simple model highlights five main purposes for learning about complexity and systems thinking. First, it helps to appreciate the complexity of organic systems, organizations, cultures, ecosystems, and human systems. Second, it helps to appreciate why mechanical, analytical approaches to change in organizations can fail. Third, to study and diagram complex systems in order to anticipate how they might respond to interventions. Fourth, it begins to embrace complexity in all its 'unknowability', instead of fearing it as most people instinctively do. Fifth, many of the issues you deal with involve both complicated and complex elements that need to be teased apart." [20]

The model introduced by Parsons deliberately uses the terms 'problem' and 'solution' in dealing with the complicated elements, and the terms 'predicament' and 'approach to addressing' in dealing with the complex elements. Let's explore the model using two personal stories

A PERSONAL COMPLICATED PROBLEM

The left side of the model describes the steps involved in dealing with a complicated challenge like writing this book. The book is a set of elements that interact together to create a story line. For example a set of elements like: the title and subtitle theme, why I wrote the book, how to use the book, my experiences, chapter introductions, sections, references and so on. The systems model instructed me to, first, *analyze* the situation, what is the theme, message, and the thread line? In addition, I did a diagnosis of what to say, what to keep and created a process to test each possible option and element. The answers came by *imagining* what the book might be, *questioning* why and how the elements could and should fit and whether each possible diagnosis made sense, and conversing with others who might have useful insight or experience. From this, I hoped to fully *analyze* the set of elements and *deduce* the most logical story line to address the writing challenges faced and the appropriate solution to each. And finally, through *collaboration* with others like my book draft reviewers, and through accepting *offers* from my editors who care about writing and flow, I *intervened* until the right writing solution was finalized. Book writing is a complicated iterative process; it is not a complex one.

A PERSONAL COMPLEX PREDICAMENT

The right side of the model, by contrast, describes the steps involved in dealing with a complex predicament like prostate cancer. Unlike my book writing challenges, I can't analyze and understand the possible causes and "fix" the problem without creating potential other predicaments. A 2008 blood test and a follow up biopsy confirmed I had early stages of prostate cancer. In my predicament all I could do was *explore* with my physician what is known (stage and scoring), and *appreciate* the complexity of the predicament and the options available, like careful watch, radiation and removal of prostate. Then, by *imagining* what might happen and the consequences of the options and having *conversations* with people who have studied the disease and people who know (have experiences) about lifestyle, and the correlations lifestyle and feelings of well-being. *Imagining and conversations* is something I have been doing since my predicament was first diagnosed in 2008 when I began a careful watch strategy that included; a set of various tests between 2008 to 2018. And through this period *collaborating and accepting offers* (advice) with the experts to stay the course, and then repeating *explore, appreciate, imagining, conversations, collaborating and accepting offers*...acknowledging the wisdom of my physician's recommendation that based on a 2018 biopsy result it was time to have my prostate removed. I had my prostate removed in May of 2018. Removal of and follow up blood work confirmed that as of today I am cancer free. Over time blood work will determine if my prostate cancer free state continues. My initial predicament and intervention has created a new predicament. A new journey has started. Today, without a prostate, my plumbing has changed. I am now learning to *adapt and work around* other aspects of my new lifestyle predicament.

Everything we do and say will remind people of the future we want to create for ourselves, our colleagues, our customers, and our organization. We will draw upon our past experiences, our core values, and our guiding purpose. We will become well-read about trends as we study the future and talk with other people about the exciting possibilities. There's no doubt that we live in interesting times, and game-changing ideas, products, and services are popping up all the time. Being part of the future allows us to contribute to its creation. We can't do that without taking time to develop our capacity to be future-focused, and we can't become future-focused without discipline and action.

While the ability to focus on the future separates leaders from the rank and file, many of us fail to understand and appreciate its importance. We devote little to no time to developing this vital quality, which then becomes a huge barrier to future success. The challenge of being forward-looking escalates with each managerial level. What are your personal thoughts about the following observations. Front-line supervisors are expected to anticipate events about three-months ahead. Mid-level managers have timelines for more complex projects and need to look three to five years into the future. What horizon should the executive suite be focused on?

Do you look beyond what's in front of you, especially when daily tasks take up so much time and energy? How are you becoming future-oriented, while handling day-to-day now challenges?

MOVING FORWARD

We generate "quick fixes" at an incredible rate, and along with a "quick fix" comes a constant stream of change re-do. Most challenges in human systems cannot be solved with a quick technical fix, regardless of how badly it is yearned for. Quick fixes lead to postponed problems. Leaders, eager to please, respond by taking a problem in hand and developing solutions that might alleviate the undesirable symptom, but not the underlying origin. A major pitfall of leadership is our assumption that we are the ones who must come up with each and every answer.

As the world becomes increasingly chaotic and unpredictable, leadership will require increased agility and an ability to adapt to both internal and external environmental conditions. There is no clear answer as to what the "right" leadership model should be. To a large extent, the culture and context in which the leader functions determine the needed model. However, when we are clear about who we are and what is important to us, our organizations have a higher probability of achieving lasting goals.

It is all too easy to revisit the same issues, engage in the same conversations, and appeal for money as the solution to all problems. Clinging to outdated processes will continue to fail us. Our job as leaders is to discover solutions best suited for the situations before us. The solutions we require are found within our own organizations. The necessary understandings we seek live within the hearts and minds of the people.

Yes, little is certain. The tempo is quicker, the dynamics are more complex, feedback loops are intense, and all within a hyper-connected world driven by a new informed customer. Leverage lies in understanding dynamic complexity and seeing inter-relationships rather than linear cause and effect chains. Leaders have an opportunity to provide strategic thinking. The skills, power, and passion required to meet this challenge *today* are present in abundance in our organizations. So, we must begin grinding out the way. We need to deal with polarities and conflicts of opposites with precision.

Let's Imagine a Future Where...

1. *Leaders are a work in progress.* They know their strengths and limitations and commit to self-reflection and improvement. They understand and display self-awareness, self-regulation, motivation, empathy, and social skills. They demonstrate integrity in their role and context and show resilience in challenging situations.

2. *Leaders enable people to engage with a vision* or goal through stories and explanations that make sense of complexity. Leaders encourage others to see and accept opportunities to contribute, learn, and grow.

3. *Leaders are people who work to make a difference.* They set a direction that is inspiring and motivating, they enable energy and effort to succeed, and they keep their eye on the goal. They work with compassion to influence the sustainability of the organization.

4. *Leaders view innovation as new opportunity.* They are passionate that there is no STATUS in the QUO.

5. *Leaders ask how they can tap into* a culture that encourages the expression of the intellect, passion, commitment, and experience of front-line workers and make real transformational changes.

6. *Leaders recognize the importance of relationships* and understand that failure to connect people leads to passive-aggressive behaviour, negative energy, a sense of hopelessness, squandering funds through inefficiencies, and above all, defeating an organization's vision.

---

7. *Leaders embrace complex, evolving organizational systems*—systems where all the parts, including services, legislation, and funding, are interconnected. A change in one of its parts has implications on the whole.

8. *Leaders recognize patterns of interdependency* and are able to explain trends and facilitate strategies that achieve maximum benefits and minimize unintended harm or negative consequences.

REFLECTIONS AND CONSIDERATIONS

What have you learned about systems, structures, and processes that provide you with the "illusion of control" and the "optics of accountability"? Do these theories reflect the realities you face?

Our proficiency at listening directly impacts our ability to lead. Do you listen openly to the ideas, opinions, comments, and criticisms of others? Do you listen to understand?

Every leader makes mistakes; fault-free leadership does not exist. How we respond and learn from our mistakes shapes our leadership development. Do you own up to, and learn from, your mistakes?

To be a good leader, at times you must be a good follower. Does your ego interrupt your ability to lead and/or follow?

Is your organization aligned and focused on delivering customer value at critical points of customer interaction? How do you infuse the culture of service throughout your organization?

With the use of technology rising, how do you ensure the human element is present? Do you look at insights and data with action-able outcomes to add value to the experience?

How much are you learning from practice? What's the last mistake you made? How did you handle it and what did you learn to do differently next time? What's one new mistake you might make this week?

How are you spending your time? Does this match your key leadership priorities? Do you have people around you who will tell you things you may not want to hear but need to hear?

Do you agree with this statement? "Your experience is real to you, and your feelings, thoughts, and wants are neither right nor wrong; they just are. Respecting and claiming your perspective while simultaneously being open to others is the key to learning."[06]

CHAPTER V
ADAPTIVE ACTION
AND LEADERSHIP

"If you don't like change, you will like irrelevance even less."
~General Eric Shinseki

INTRODUCTION

Adaptive action is about incremental pragmatism and dealing with polarities and conflicts of opposites with precision. It is about execution, momentum, focus, finish, and finding the balance for speed and need for engagement. It includes setting direction; strategically aligning decisions to vision, values, and evidence; taking action to implement results; and assessing and evaluating outcomes. Adaptive action is not a destination, but a way of being where improvement is built on connected and overlapping principles that promote a foundation consisting of the worker's voice, leader's ears, and organizational support. To say it another way, it's about how reflection fuels, people matter, and relationships make the difference

In this chapter I set the conditions for adaptive leadership action. A story of adaptive action coupled with a metaphor brings the people and relationship threads together. A discussion about resiliency, blurring lines and competing tensions sets the stage for a conversation about change principles and renewal.

PROBLEMS AND PARADOXES

Solving problems follow a predictable pattern: highlight an issue, gather the facts, investigate causes, formulate solutions, and implement the answer. The objective is to gain control. If we fail, we cast blame on others and ourselves. What do we do when there are paradoxes without easy solutions? Here are some examples: Should we focus on the short or long-term initiatives? Do we invest in new business initiatives or maximize profits from existing businesses? Do we centralize or decentralize operations? Do we hold individuals or entire teams accountable for results?

Paradoxes are not solved; paradoxes are managed. The challenge for CEOs, boards of directors, and other senior leaders is how to manage paradoxes and refrain from applying problem-solving approaches to them. In his book, *Big Winners and Big Losers*, Professor Marcus found that few organizations are long-term winners over a ten-year period. "Only about three percent of companies outperform their industry's average, while about six percent will underperform the average. Leaders of winning organizations do a great job of managing paradoxes. Achieving a proper balance among competing elements, they weave competing tendencies together rather than emphasizing one pole in a paradox over the other. For instance, managing the built-in tension of achieving short-term profitability and sustaining long-term competitive advantage requires balancing agility and openness to change with the focus and discipline of execution. Long-term success requires the exploration for new markets, products and services and at the same time, exploitation of existing products, services and other capabilities."[1]

One of the most powerful of all paradoxes is that an unattainable goal may well be the only goal worth working toward. Indeed, is this not the purpose of leadership? To quote Carl Jung: "All the greatest and most important problems of life are fundamentally insoluble. They must be so, for they express the necessary polarity in every self-regulating system. They can never be solved, but only outgrown."[2]

Balancing the polarity is a remarkable engineering and architectural achievement in organizational re-design. Each individual within the organization has the potential to undermine or create positive dynamics at any point in time. Each person can regard any issue as an uncoordinated, disconnected process, or as a challenge. A great test of organizational maturity is recognizing and taking responsibility for the reality we create, that our world will be as we see it, and that the effectiveness of the organization will arise from millions of moments of interpretation.

In Chapter III, under multidimensional relationships, we discussed the importance of "going to the dance floor." Let's use the metaphor of "on the balcony of personal reflection" above the "dance floor" to depict what it means to gain the distanced perspective we need to see what is really happening. If we stay moving on the dance floor, all we will see will be the people dancing with and around us. Swept up in the music, it may be a great party, but our perspective is limited. If we move up to the balcony, we may see a very different picture. When we move back and forth between balcony and dance floor, we can continually assess what is happening in our organization and take corrective midcourse action. If we perfect this skill, we might even be able to do both simultaneously, keeping one eye on the events happening around us and the other eye on the larger patterns and dynamics. The great sports athletes like Wayne Gretzky have the ability to simultaneously be in the moment and see where the play is going to end up. Later we will introduce hockey as a metaphor for adaptive change

Now the backend of the Jung quote from above: "This outgrowing, as I formerly called it, on further experience was seen to consist in a new level of consciousness. Some higher or wider interest arose on the horizon, and through this widening of view; the insoluble problem lost its urgency. It was not solved logically in its own terms but faded out when confronted with a new and stronger image."[2]

The LEGO museum in Billund Denmark has an exhibit that lists eleven paradoxes of today's leadership. Lego is a building block. You start with an image of what success looks like and you use the building blocks interchangeably. Instructions are only so helpful. It's more fun when more people are working together to create and build. Imagination is a key input alongside two simple words, what if.

Eleven Paradoxes of Leadership

1. To be able to establish close relationship with your employees – and to keep proper distance

2. To take the lead – and to recede into the background

3. To show the employee confidence – and to be aware of their doings

4. To be tolerant – and to know how you want things done

5. To be concerned about your own field of responsibility – and at the same time to be loyal to the overall goals of the company

6. To plan your working day carefully – and to be flexible to your planning

7. To express your opinion – and to be diplomatic

8. To be visionary – and to keep both feet firmly on the ground

9. To aim at consensus – and to be able to cut through

10. To be dynamic – but also thoughtful

11. To be self-confident – and humble [3]

Each of the eleven paradoxes builds on the ones that come before and after it. Values and guiding principles for an organization often exist in a polarity between their positive and negative expression. We publicly proclaim the ideal organization as an expression of new integration and organizing rules, but this does not eliminate their negative expression. Trust is a magnificent value, but when the talk is not walked, people face risk. The opposite, or negative, can never be eliminated, only contained. At a certain point many organizations begin to crack under the pressure of the two extended poles on the continuum of values. Unless, people develop a way to transmute the lead of organizational culture into the gold of the organizational vision.

Adaptive action is an iterative process involving key activities: observing events and learning patterns around you, interpreting what you are observing and developing multiple hypothesis about what is really going on, and designing interventions based on observations and interpretations to address the adaptive challenge identified.

The organization must be open to the prospect for new businesses beyond its core and defend the positions it presently holds. Successful leaders manage this paradox well and achieve improved long-term success.

Sorting through an adaptive challenge takes time and reflection. What paradoxes in leadership have you observed? Which are the toughest for you?

INTER-CONNECTED ADAPTIVE ACTIVITIES AND ACTION

Adaptive action is gathering data and information to make meaning out of what we know and taking action to shift the patterns and see what happens. Adaptive leadership mobilizes our greatest asset, our people, and leverages relationships to outgrow the present paradoxes and problems. As Jung says: "Confront with a new ands stronger image."[2]

Peter Senge framed it this way: "By coming together in an open and honest dialogue, we can integrate our fragmented individual snapshot perceptions to bring focus into a more complete and accurate representation of a shared reality."[4] We ought to resist the pressure to do something and spend more time diagnosing the problem, even if taking that much time feels uncomfortable. We must assess our own skills and determine whether we are the right person to intervene or if someone else would have a better chance of success.

L. Ledoux's "Synthesis of the book...Practice of Adaptive Leadership" suggests that in order to be an adaptive leader, there are at least four pre-conditions.

GET RID OF THE BROKEN SYSTEM'S ILLUSION

"There is a myth that drives many change initiatives into the ground: that the organization needs to change because it is broken. The reality is that any social system is the way it is because the people in that system want it that way. In that sense, on the whole, on balance, the system is working fine, even though it may appear to be "dysfunctional" in some respects to some members and outside observers, even though it faces danger just over the horizon. There is no such thing as a dysfunctional organization, because every organization is perfectly aligned to achieve the results it currently gets. No one who tries to name or address the dysfunction in an organization will be popular. When you realize that what you see as dysfunctional works for others in the system, you begin focusing on how to mobilize and sustain people through the period of risk that often comes with adaptive change, rather than trying to convince them of the rightness of your cause.

LEARN TO LIVE IN THE DISEQUILIBRIUM

"To practice adaptive leadership, you have to help people navigate through a period of disturbance as they sift through what is essential and what is expendable and as they experiment with solutions to the adaptive challenges at hand. You need to be able to do two things: (1) manage yourself in that environment and (2) help people tolerate the discomfort they are experiencing.

ENGAGE ABOVE AND BELOW THE NECK

"If leadership involves will and skill, then leadership requires the engagement of what goes on both above and below the neck. Courage requires all of you: heart, mind, spirit, and guts. Skill requires learning new competencies, with your brain training your body to become proficient at new techniques of diagnosis and action.

CONNECT TO PURPOSE

"It makes little sense to practice leadership and put your own professional success and material gain at risk unless it is on behalf of some larger purpose that you find compelling. What might such a purpose look like? How can you tell whether a particular purpose is worth the risks involved in leading adaptive change in your organization? Clarifying the values that orient your life and work and identifying purposes to which you might commit are courageous acts. You have to choose among competing, legitimate purposes, sacrificing many in the service of one or a few. In doing so, you make a statement about what you are willing to die for, and therefore, what you are willing to live for"[5]

Four Conditions For Adaptive Leadership In Action

Building on the four pre-conditions for adaptive leadership, Ron Heifetz, renowned expert on adaptive leadership, suggests that "the practice of adaptive leadership consists of four inter-connected activities; diagnosing the system, mobilizing the system, seeing yourself as a system, and deploying yourself."[6]

What follows is a story about change illustrating the four inter-connected adaptive leadership activities. A complete version of the story is captured in an article by M. Fenn titled "Reinvigorating Publicly Funded Medicare in Ontario: New Public Policy and Public Administration Techniques."[7] As cited in the article as executive lead for the new public policy and public administration approach, I made many contributions to the following storyline of four inter-connected adaptive activities.

DIAGNOSING THE SYSTEM

"In 2004 healthcare consumed nearly half the Ontario provincial budget and the Ministry of Health and Long-Term Care had grown into a vast and segmented organization where individual divisions had closer links to their divisional health sector stakeholders than to other parts of the healthcare system or parts of the Ontario government.

Leaders within individual healthcare provider organizations (e.g., physicians, nurses, hospital presidents, long-term care home operators, pharmaceutical firms, etc.) had become very adept at making direct and individualized approaches to political leadership and to senior ministry executives. In this context, there was doubt surrounding the ability of the health ministry to lead a fundamental, strategic and long-term reform of the existing healthcare system; a system they had invested in and were intimately interwoven into.

Could government disengage from the daily hurly-burly of crisis management in order to conceive and execute a fundamental system-wide reform, especially if it entailed a diminution of is traditional pre-eminent and hands-on role?

In the run up to the 2003 provincial election, opposition leader Dalton McGuinty and key political advisers began to consider the experience of other leaders (such as Tony Blair and Bill Clinton), as they took office facing major challenges. The subsequent victory of the McGuinty Liberals, on a platform that featured health, education, and energy, suddenly faced an unanticipated large budgetary deficit. This deficit brought healthcare reform to the top of their agenda.

Strategically, the Ontario government proposed to deduce the issues of complexity and interrelatedness down to a manageable number of generally understood terms that would provide clear system transforming targets and outcomes. The Ontario government proposed to enlist a wider ensemble, local public, and new players into the planning and reform processes.

In an organic system like the health sector, undisturbed existing structures and internal processes (which created the existing system and on which it was based) are relied upon to create (or recreate) a modification of the existing models, but not to create significantly new constructs. The Ontario government believed a more machined and streamlined version of existing processes would not achieve sought-after goals. The system required entirely new processes." [7]

Are you ready to observe and interpret before intervening? Are you including in your observation and interpretation the following; the human system itself, the adaptive challenge, the political landscape, and the qualities that make a human organization adaptive?

MOBILIZING THE SYSTEM

"With a reform philosophy in place, the Ontario government sought a unique organizational mechanism to secure stakeholder support/consent for action and a strategy to execute. It proposed to use information management and information technology, in part to go over the heads of the healthcare's institutional voices to engage their colleagues and the broader public as allies in reform. It sought to demystify the nature and problems of the system and illustrate the performance of healthcare practitioners and the component parts of the healthcare system.

Information management would be employed in a fresh way. Some members of the new government thought the institutional opposition had stymied many earlier, poorly articulated reform efforts. It reasoned that a sophisticated provider/stakeholder audience, generally trained in scientific method, would be more likely to accept empirical evidence drawn from their own reporting. The provider/stakeholder would also be more likely to listen to peers rather than, or before, government bureaucrats, politicians, and economists. Good information management and data analyses would support the diagnosis, prognosis, and prescriptions to reinvigorate their healthcare system—a system where public policy and public finance arguments had limited effect on those who had to undergo and lead the necessary changes.

The significance of information went beyond its content. New information forced bureaucrats and providers out of their comfortable assumptions and their traditional roles as custodians of the wisdom. All the players in the healthcare system were compelled to listen afresh to the voice of the patient. New transparent information reframed the customary discussion and forced reconsideration of conventional professional wisdom and traditional nostrums.

Basically, government identified the end-state destination and then let the system participants choose the route. As long as the direction was clear and progress assessed empirically, the corollary of this approach enlisted the participants within the healthcare system to reform and re-engineer their own system.

The Ontario government proposed to alter the ground rules that traditionally framed the healthcare debate. The government wanted to change the relationship among the participants by introducing a facilitator and catalyst." [7]

Are you with others making and generating multiple interpretations and designing effective interventions? Are you orchestrating necessary conflict, and building an adaptive culture?

SEEING YOURSELF AS A SYSTEM

"In conventional Canadian public administration, a newly elected government achieves its new political agenda by enlisting the impartial public service in elaborating policy options, or the agenda is preordained by a detailed electoral campaign platform that enlists the public service to implement the policy directions of the new government.

The new Ontario government faced a dilemma. On one hand, it had a clear, sincere, and public commitment to a strong and impartial civil service. On the other hand, there was a perception that key elements of the government's political agenda might be at risk if it were entrusted to ministries whose bureaucracies might be institutionally or culturally constrained from delivering the government's agenda.

The doubt surrounding the civil services' ability to deliver might lie elsewhere in the bureaucracy. Internal processes for accountability and coordination had become voluminous, ponderous, and complex over the past three decades. Some suggested the civil service and successive governments had created for themselves a skein of central agency processes, procedures, and committees—a skein so daunting it threatened to suffocate the potential for creativity and innovation on the part of line ministries.

With advice from its cabinet secretary and senior political and civil service staff, the new Ontario government decided to take a whole new organizational approach with its mandate. The government opted to respect the principles of an independent civil service and non-partisan civil service leadership to implement key reforms. The government also decided to free system reform leadership of many traditional bureaucratic responsibilities. It sought to supplement civil service leadership with outsiders and experts commissioned to champion time sensitive results. It aimed to ensure decision-making was decisive and done in real time, without the confusing and cumbersome policy approval processes of ministries and cabinet. The government was determined to provide close political monitoring and counsel.

The results agenda approach was borrowed from Britain's Blair government. In the case of health reform, the team was known as the Health Results Team (or with a mild touch of healthcare irony, "HRT"). This organizational model established a parallel decision-making organism within government that diverted much of the traditional and often sclerotic ministerial policy development and central agency/cabinet committee review processes.

The foundation of the HRT model was made up of dedicated civil service leadership, including several senior ministry civil servants with a reputation for achievement. These individuals were placed in essentially non-ministerial roles. The HRT model gave equal status representation to political staff from the health minister's office and the premier's office. It also added outside experts drawn from the healthcare field, who were charged with championing and/or validating key initiatives in the reform strategy." [7]

Identify who you are, know you triggers, expectations, and your personal hard drive, broaden your tolerances and articulate and connect everything to purpose.

DEPLOYING YOURSELF

"The HRT was best known for its single-minded and inspirational devotion to the time-limited results agenda. The HRT pioneered a novel and sophisticated implementation strategy, which focused on engaging and leveraging a wide array of participants to achieve the promises of healthcare reform.

Having secured the mandate to recruit and deploy staff, government was persuaded to give responsibility for individual reform portfolios to leaders with equally non-stereotypical pedigrees and assignments. Serving as part of the HRT apparatus these leaders and experts who were distinct from the ministry proper could challenge traditional assumptions and institutional resistance more easily and in a manner that was largely unavailable to traditional ministry executives. They possessed a credibility that stakeholders could not deny and grew to respect further.

The HRT model shifted much of the governmental policy and decision-making processes from within the ministry and cabinet committees to an alternative forum with direct and frequent access to the most senior political and civil service leadership. HRT met monthly with the premier and utilized a unique set of briefing materials to guide those decision-making sessions. The leadership of the HRT was time-limited and externally led, with few routine responsibilities. The main body of the ministry dealt with the daily business of running Ontario's demanding $33-billion healthcare system and responded to present chronic distractions and issues during reform implementation.

The HRT initiative had several other unique characteristics. First, it developed and championed a defined group of policy initiatives. It designated results as the political and operational measure of its success. Second, it operationalized the philosophy of organic organizational reform. It embraced the concepts of leverage, expertise, information transparency, and momentum to offset the traditional impediments to healthcare reform. Traditional impediments were inherent in governmental decision-making processes. The organic structural reforms were specifically designed to compel the system to open itself to new models of behaviour and decision-making.

The HRT bolstered its ability to carry out its strategy by appointing leaders who had sufficient professional and personal autonomy to say what needed to be said. Care would be taken to develop a storyline with a focus on outcomes, which was developed and used to broadcast a clear, consistent, and engaging message to stakeholders and the broader community. This communications approach used all available channels, including stakeholder conferences and strategically chosen meetings with health ministry executives, system stakeholders, and political leadership and their staff.

Reform was needed in a wide range of clinical and operational areas, and the use of leverage was essential to create early momentum. The HRT used expert panels to enlist expertise, common understanding, and not coincidentally, to go over the heads of those most likely to mount institutional resistance. For their part, the expert panels had the latitude and the mandate to pose questions not routinely posed by those in and running the healthcare system. With a well-defined visioning for key areas, the directional questions became more obvious and appropriate." [7]

My experiences with this work confirmed the following: stay grounded and connected to purpose, engage courageously, inspire people, run experiments, take risks, and thrive on the action. "After observing the events, patterns and context around you, give yourself license to assess your own skills and to determine if you are the right person to intervene or someone else would have a better chance of success." [6]

In the increasingly complex and horizontal organizational environment of decision-making, the ability of organizations to advance major new initiatives can be compromised or impeded by the cumbersome systems evolved to ensure both due diligence and a comprehensive approach. Often what is absent is the table-setting conditions for adaptive leadership and change.

"Adaptive leadership takes you out of your daily routine to unknown territory requiring ways of acting that are outside your repertoire, with no guarantee of your competence or your success. There is a bit of paradox here. On one hand, you are trying to lead on behalf of something you believe in that is beyond your individual interest. On the other hand, in order to be most effective in doing so, you need to pay attention to how you manage, use, and deploy yourself. Its not self-indulgence, it is smart personal leadership."[5]

Are you moving back and forth between the balcony and the dance floor? Are you continually assessing what is happening in your unit and organization?

How are you developing your adaptive leadership skills?

RATIONAL, FORMATIVE AND TRANSFORMATIVE APPROACHES TO CHANGE

Transformation in attitude, understanding, and behaviour is an experience. Real 'transformation' reveals what is true now, the ideal solution to meet the evolutionary need in an organizational system now, and the pathway to what is now universally true. The wisdom of many knowledge traditions says that truth is multi-dimensional, and it contains and balances opposing forces.

Consider how you would answer the following questions: Is the future known or unknown? What causes an organization to move into the future? When transformative change occurs, what exactly is changing?

Stacey, Griffin, and Shaw, in *Complexity and Management: Fad or Radical Challenge to Systems Thinking*, suggest that those who believe in control and prediction will think and act in very different ways from those who believe that the future is unknown, and thus, unpredictable. Many will believe that the future is both known and unknown. To examine this further, let's take a look at three approaches that they suggest determine how an organization becomes what it is.

RATIONAL APPROACH

"The basic assumption is that organizational movement is toward a known and predictable future. There is a strong belief that a known future arrives via various methods of control, such as the use of established performance measures, rational analyses, plans, goals, and actions of leaders and managers. There is no self-organization present, so stability and change are the result of choices made by autonomous human beings scrutinizing and planning on behalf of the organization. Motivation of the workforce is critical to realize the chosen aim and strategic goals. Statements of mission, vision, and established universal values are essential so that all employees are singing from the same hymnbook.

FORMATIVE APPROACH

The assumption here is that movement is toward a future that is known or predictable by the interaction of an organization's related parts. The organization self-organizes to reveal a predictable future. Time is from a given past toward a present. The future is recognizable from the past and the past is carried forward in the present to the desired future. It is a deterministic view that realizes a future through the unfolding of the past into the present. Helping employees, thus the organization, realize their full potential assumes that the potential already exists in the form (employees). The final form (organization) is realized by the maturation of agents' selves or organizational identity that was already present.

TRANSFORMATIVE APPROACH

Assumes that movement to a future state is caused by self-organization that occurs in the micro-interactions of organizational life in which each moment is influenced by previous moments. Each moment is a reconstruction of the past in the present, accompanied by simultaneous continuity and change in the present, as the future is continually under construction—an unknown and unpredictable future."[8]

Hockey a Metaphor for Adaptive Action

Put yourself in the place of a spectator at a hockey game. You arrive full of confidence that your favourite team, who has had a good record of wins this year, will not disappoint you. The players on both teams are highly trained and skilled. Based on a close evaluation of tapes from previous games, coaches and players arrive convinced that they understand the strengths and weaknesses of the other team. With their analyses complete and a strategy determined, a game plan has been drawn. Coaches and players alike are well prepared, having been instructed on all game strategies.

The idea of the game is that each player and team must navigate a way through the game that will guarantee a win. The win is obviously the desired outcome. The stakes are high as reputations are on the line. Money, energy, and fan support are invested in achieving a win.

You are part of the crowd of spectators and have come to the game filled with confidence in your team. The hockey arena represents the environment and the society that surrounds it. The way in which the game is played represents the assumptions, beliefs, behaviours, and practices of hockey players. The way the game is played out also represents various choices that need to be made by the actors within the action. Training, skill, and expertise represent the past; the game represents the present; and the win at the other side of the game represents the desired future. Will the tactical plan developed prior to the game lead to the desired future?

Meuser and MacLeod in an essay titled "Lessons from the Stanley Cup Playoffs" use the metaphor of a hockey game to illustrate the elements of rational, formative and transformative approaches.

"*In a rational approach*, attention is turned toward the team's coaches. These are the individuals who create the strategic maps for the players. They do this by analysis of previous games, and by evaluation of each player's skills and competencies, as well as past performance. They move players around the map in a way that they, the rational decision-makers, deem necessary for the win. Before the game begins and as it progresses, decisions and choices about the game are the responsibilities of the coaches. Therefore, any necessary changes in strategy are discussed with players before and during the game as a result of observations and conclusions made by the observant coach. There is no self-organization, and whether the team wins or loses is accredited to coaches. Loss is the fault of the coaches for failing to adequately train and/or motivate their team.

The assumption is that those external to the action, the rational observers, can best determine the plans and actions necessary to win the game. Change is a result of rational choice. The problem with this approach is the map may simply be wrong. Assumptions made at the beginning of the game cannot account for all the possible eventualities. If the game is not what was expected, a rationalist approach may lead the coaches to continue in spite of what is happening around the game and within the players on the field. A rationalist approach trusts that, if the players implement the plans and designs of their coaches/managers and team owners, the goal will be successfully reached.

"Within a formative approach, players will have been given the strategic map prior to the game. They will have done their homework, attended all pre-game coaching sessions, and will have been given a strategy to follow. Like a rational approach, this approach is based on past performance of the team as well as the perceived performance of the other team.

Players will put their uniforms on and proceed to the ice with a belief that, if the map/plan is correct, all that is required is to unfold the plans and designs of the coaches, team, follow the rules and principles of hockey, and release their own potential. A win is assured. They may or may not have had input into the plan, but nonetheless, with their skill and training, they can quite competently bring home the win. Whether the game is won or lost, formative approach informs that the whole (game) is already contained within the rules of interaction of the parts in the macro processes of repetition and iteration that will unfold the mature form of the game and the outcome.

A formative approach assumes that the team will self-organize within the game, repeating and adapting pre-given forms and strategies. Players will adapt their play, but there will be no significant transformation of the strategies or the players. Consequently, the map could fail and the game lost. Losing may place the season in jeopardy for the team. The greater desired outcome, the win, will be out of reach. No doubt the players will be blamed, or traded.

"A transformative approach is interested in everything that is happening in and around the ice surface—the players, coaches, spectators, ice conditions, temperature, and so forth. The players find themselves in a complex game situation where a map is useless. There are game rules and a rule of conduct for fairness and safety, but due to the circumstances within the play, the pre-game map is insufficient. The outcome of the game is unpredictable and uncontrollable. The whole situation on the ice is self-organizing and non-determined. No one in the stands or on the ice knows how the game will be played out or what the final score will be.

The players are self-organizing according to the micro-interactions between, within, and among them in the living present. Constraint and free will are inherent within their interaction and participation. There are also micro-diversity and fluctuations in how players experience and find meaning within the competition. Constraint and freedom are articulated as conflict and co-operation, and are simultaneously acting on the play action, the game is held within a paradox of stability and instability at the same time.

No individual player or team of players is in control of the interaction; no individual player or team can decide or intend for others. In the heat of the action, the coach behind the bench is incapable of planning and controlling the event. The future of the game is continually under construction in the living present due to the personal, social, physical, and psychological freedom players bring to their micro-interactions and participation. The dynamic of the game is emergent within the context of micro-diversity and small fluctuations in play.

All players continually choose and intend for themselves in the moment. Being seasoned players, they recognize the emerging patterns of play; they differentiate between similarities and differences from other hockey games. The patterns that they are acting within are emergent, arising from all players' continual interaction. These patterns of micro-interaction are continually forming and being formed by them. Essentially, they are all engaged in a process of simultaneous intuitive and reflective practice: They are sensing and reflecting on and in each play. They are participants and observers at the same time. Meaning, choice and intention all emerge in the living present. Therefore, teammates and teams are continually forming the game while being formed by it, perpetually constructing and reconstructing the future.

No one player can decide for another or for his or her team. But, the interplay of expertise, diversity, power, constraint and interaction has the potential to produce unexpected and often unwelcome outcomes. The centrality of self-organizing interaction causes new variations to emerge within the game action and potentially the game of hockey itself.

As players are choosing for themselves alone within the play action, another paradox inheres. Every player is simultaneously in a process of continuity and change, as are the teams, coaches, spectators and game. In transformative approach, continuity and change are occurring at the same time: There is an *opportunity* for continuity or for transformation to a novel state, but without a *guarantee*. In essence, each player and team is in a place of potentiality wherein their individual and collective identities, and differences, are being continually expressed, but with no guarantee of continuity or transformation of those identities. If transformative change occurs, the players and the teams remain paradoxically the same, yet different. In transformative, it is the player's identity as well as the identities of the organization, spectator, team and environment that can change."[9]

Managing complexity does not mean that rational and formative approaches are without value.

How are you leading within the paradoxical notion of all interconnection and participation of rational, formative and transformative approaches to change?

RESILIENCY

The discussion about the dynamics of a hockey game and the four groups of interconnected activity for adaptive action provides an important opportunity to discuss resilience engineering and its application to a number of key issues confronting organizations today. Effectiveness, efficiency, quality, safety, and customer experience are only a few issues we face today.

Resiliency is the ability to persevere when difficulties arise. Resilient leaders are persistent and able to cope with setbacks. Resiliency is the ability to learn from your mistakes and bounce back with renewed commitment to your vision.

In the last decade, resilience engineering has become a key conceptual and practical approach to these issues. Resilience acknowledges the dynamic nature of this work much like the dynamics of a hockey game, and the intrinsic capacity of an organization, its component parts, and its people to adjust prior to, during, and after dynamic disturbances to maintain required operations under both expected and unexpected conditions.

Shep, Cardiff, and MacLeod, in an essay titled "Resiliency: Time for Change." suggest that the "resilience perspective is an exemplar of the transformational approach described in the hockey metaphor. It focuses on the dynamic interactions among people doing the work, as well as between people and organizations. It recognizes how design is the starting point for examining how work is accomplished. It provides greater insight into understanding how learning is created in complex adaptive systems.

"Given the inevitability in any dynamic system for the unexpected (i.e. surprises), resilience thinking has identified four capabilities organizations require to maintain reasonable stability in the face of change: to learn tolerance from past events; to monitor current conditions and threats; to respond to regular and irregular conditions flexibly; and to anticipate long term threats, challenges and opportunities.

By placing emphasis on how everyday work gets done, a deeper understanding of organizational work is revealed. It provides a broader and deeper sense of how critical incidents occur. It poses questions that lead to a greater capacity in understanding and fosters an appreciation for variation." [10]

Petrie, in a white paper titled "Wake Up!" [11] suggests four steps to building resilience:

BE PRESENT

"Be aware of where you are and what you are doing right now. Stop dreaming so much about the past and the future. Athletes, surgeons, or artists all talk about a state of mind they enter when they are at their best. They talk about how time slows down, they are completely present to the task, and their mind stops wandering. Everything just seems to happen naturally and many report that they are simply watching themselves do the task." [11] Psychologists call it "the zone" or a "state of flow." [12] These high performers find it hard to explain, but they know exactly how it feels. If you have experienced it, then you also know how it feels. It feels like being wide awake.

CONTROL YOUR ATTENTION

"The key to controlling your attention is to practice consciously putting your attention where you want it to be and holding it there. Once you notice that ruminating thoughts are snatching it away, simply acknowledge that your mind has wandered, e.g. thinking about tomorrow's meeting. Then bring your mind back to the present moment. Practice this again and again." [11]

"Charismatic leaders understand the power of attention. Bill Clinton is famous for his ability to deeply connect with people within seconds due to his determination to give them his full, undivided attention. He is said to have the ability to make each person feel like he/she is the only person in the room.[13]

DETACH

"Detachment is the ability to get appropriate distance from the situations you are facing. In my experience, people who score highest on detachment do two things extremely well. First, they maintain perspective. They don't turn molehills into mountains, meaning they don't let situations overwhelm them. Second, they focus on what they can control[11]

LET GO

"At the core of why we continue to ruminate about things long after they have happened is that we refuse to let go. The leaders who are best at letting go are those who ask themselves a simple question: Will continuing to focus on this help me, my people, or my organization?"[11] If the answer is no, they let it go. A classic example of letting go is Nelson Mandela, who when asked why he was not angrier about spending half his life in jail replied, "If I thought it would be useful, I would be."[14]

I invite you to reflect on the way you get your work done, and in particular to think back on a moment of success amidst what, on all accounts, could have been a disaster. Step back and consider the following: What is it that you and your colleagues (if team dynamics are relevant in your example) were doing? How did you manage to create a good outcome, despite the circumstances? Can you describe why you think things turned out well?

BLURRING LINES AND COMPETING TENSIONS

Think about the burring lines between technology and the human element, causing us to rethink work. Think about the ongoing changes to multiple organizational structures. Think about work place wellness and harmony, shifting roles and responsibilities, and the multi-generational workforce. Think about the rapid pace of research and evidence, and knowledge transfer on these topics. Think about the need for nimble organizational priority setting, and policy making that keeps up with change, rapid risk analysis, and recalibration.

What is clear is that organizational life has changed, and will continue to change. Ron Heifetz, in *Adaptive Learning*, suggests the true test of leaders is in the manner in which they respond to adaptive problems with competing tensions, those problems that challenge us to learn and act in an entirely new way of "being" and "doing."[15] Most crises in human systems cannot be solved with an easy technical fix. Nonetheless, people usually want leaders to answer with a "quick fix."

What does this mean for the lines between research, evaluation, and organizational improvement? All these traditions need to focus on developing a new kind of evidence base that supports adaptation and learning. The world of evaluation is giving rise to an important new idea: shared value through shared measurement. Shared measurement requires a common platform for data capture and analysis. When participants get to define measures together, a shared measurement platform enables comparative performance. When participation is ongoing, this platform can be used to create systems of influence and an environment of adaptive learning through collective efforts—an environment that can measure, learn, coordinate, and improve performance.

Academic researchers are developing new science in domains such as "research on knowledge translation" and "dissemination and implementation science." This development has given rise to published research on scalability and evidence-based de-implementation for contradicted and unproven organizational practices.

These new areas of study acknowledge the extraneous variables that cannot be controlled. New processes must be applied in order to understand extraneous variables and how they impact process and outcomes. Breaking down the silos between research, evaluation, and quality improvement might help us move beyond the now.

The boundaries of research, organizational operations, and policy-making must intersect. Together, we can bring to the surface the assumptions we hold by tackling odious system problems. We need to consider the assumptions, actions, and choices at many different levels if we want to recognize patterns and differences in our collective thought. These patterns and differences can be used to discover common ground and/or to find creative alternatives for stubborn organizational problems.

An essay by Finegood and MacLeod titled "Blurring the Lines Between Research, Evaluation and Outcome" raises a number of questions. "What is the difference between research and evaluation? There are many different answers to this question. Some will say that research is what you do when you plan up front, while evaluation is what you do after the fact. Others may declare that research has no client, and evaluation does. Some fail to distinguish a difference between the two terms. Our understanding of these two terms is better defined when we expand the question to include quality improvement or ask more nuanced questions, such as When would it be good to blur the lines of research and evaluation and when should they be kept clear?

Many of the differences seem artificial and unhelpful, such as the notion that evaluators require a unique set of skills or the idea that theory is more important in research than evaluation. Another argument central to the research and evaluation fray is that research creates generalizable new knowledge while program evaluation and quality improvement provides informing decisions and identifies improvements in internal processes and practices.

The growing complexity of life in our highly networked and technology-driven world can be at the heart of both future despair and future hope. Maintaining clear distinctions between research, evaluation, and organizational improvement means reinforced silos. The majority of research today adheres to a reductionist paradigm where we try to control or measure all extraneous variables considered to be relevant. In program evaluation, the culture uses multiple lines of evidence to answer questions and minimize confounding results. In organizational improvement, the tradition is to acknowledge extraneous variables but not to interfere. When presented with an odious challenge, a reductionist approach is no longer helpful. Complete control of extraneous variables is impossible to achieve, and even partial control offers results that may not be applicable in the real world. Control is linked to the notion there is only one "real truth." [16]

Many leaders, eager to please, respond accordingly by taking the problem on their shoulders and coming up with solution that will typically alleviate a symptom, not the underlying issue. Heifetz points out that "a major pitfall of leadership is assuming that somehow you're the one who's got to come up with the answers rather than develop the adaptive capacity, the capacity of people, to face hard problems and take responsibility for them." [15]

Adaptive leadership involves raising tough questions, rather than providing answers; it means framing the issues in a way that encourages people to think differently. Adaptive leadership means co-creating new roles with those who will fill them.

Adaptive leadership means orchestrating conflict between the silos of research, policy, and operations, rather than quelling it. Conflict is a tremendous source of creativity. Heifetz points out that "leaders in the midst of adaptive change must be able to artfully guide their people through a balance of disorientation and new learning. They need to hold the group in an optimal state of tension and disequilibrium that stimulates a quest for learning, without jarring people so much that they simply are not able to learn."[10] Dissatisfaction with the status quo is the first step toward progress.

Robert Fritz, author of *The Path of Least Resistance,* says, "as complex adaptive systems undergo multiple change dynamics, the tension in the system will either be rooted in creativity and innovations, or, it will be rooted in fear and anxiety."[17]

In a dissipative structure, anything that disturbs the system plays a crucial role in helping it self-organize into a new form. Whenever an environment offers new and different information, the system chooses whether or not to accept the provocation and respond. New information might only be a slight variation from the norm, but a variation of any magnitude can hold the seed for significant change. If the information becomes a large enough disturbance within the system, real change can occur. At this moment, the system is jarred by internal disturbance and is far from equilibrium. The system is incapable of working with new information; it cannot deal with the disturbance and therefore dissolves it. This integration does not signal the death of the system. If a living system can maintain its identity, it can self-organize to a higher level of complexity—a new form of itself that can deal better with the present.

A leader must constantly balance polarities associated with realism and idealism. This careful balancing act is a tremendous challenge. This paradox creates unending predicaments in terms of managing the short-term with the long-term. If the immediate is ignored, there will be no future to worry about. However, if concern for the long-term is disregarded, future success is left to chance. Living in realism means dealing with facts, certainty, order, and a short-term horizon. On the other hand, living in idealism means coping with uncertainties, chaos, and the intangible and unexpected. Leadership has both a strategic and a personal side. It must be rooted in both vision and reality, where vision is a way of thinking proactively and reality provides the immediate context in terms of being connected with the external environment and internal actuality.

When we were hunter-gatherers, a simple control structure with one clear leader for each organizational structure was quite adequate. As we passed from early civilizations through the industrial revolution, more complicated and hierarchical control structures were required. But with the advent of the Internet and the current technological revolution, we need networked control structures, which enable more local action and authority, since top-down control is no longer effective. All hands (researchers, evaluators and system performance leaders) are needed on deck to transform our human systems to ones designed for this increasingly complex world we are living in. In complex systems individuals matter and we need to engage everyone in ways we can successfully make decisions we need to make in our corner of this complex world.

As a leader are you provocative and open to alternatives? Do you invite inquiry and bring to the surface the fundamental issues that need to be addressed? Do you engage in a new dialogue that seeks interdependent solutions to research, policy, and organizational challenges?

CHANGE PRINCIPLES

My leadership learning experiences with change provided an opportunity to test and fully appreciate that there are several placements on which you can find yourself on the face of a transformation-change wave. If you are too far ahead, the wave will crash down and you will be at the mercy of its violent surge. If you are tentative and fail to harness the available energy, you run the risk of being left behind. If you place yourself in perfect trim and continue to make adjustments, you can actually ride the wave. Discovering where you need to be allows you to become one with the wave.

Leadership is about exhibiting courage and boldness to maneuver through the present turbulence and pandemonium. Being bold requires perseverance, commitment, confidence, and strength of character. It requires a certain amount of "stick-to-it-iveness." As the transformational waves peak and subside, the leader needs to chart the course, ride each wave with finesse and conviction, and ultimately stay focused on the end game. Flexibility and dexterity are required to conquer the waves of change and to navigate a new course if necessary. The following five connected and overlapping principles impact the riding and ability to adapt to transformational change waves.

SHARED CLARITY OF PURPOSE

Clarity of purpose is what happens when a group of individuals align their belief systems or values with a common challenge, vision, or goal. Purpose taps into people's need for meaningful work and to be part of something bigger than us. It encapsulates people's cognitive and emotional commitment to a cause. Clarity of purpose is not just 'nice to have,' but a critical driver of success in performance improvement and change. This is particularly true of large-scale change in complex organizations. A clear purpose with unified goals reduces the emergence of sub-agendas that can lead to silo and turf wars. Strong relationships foster the communication necessary to create networks and the emergence of new ideas, practices, and systems. Strong relationships thrive in an environment/culture that is accompanied with trust and respect. Without clarity of purpose it is difficult if not impossible to adequately align efforts.

ALIGNMENT OF EFFORT

A smooth operating system is not the product of a series of isolated actions, but rather stems from orchestrating the right combination of interactions at the right time for the right person in the right places. However, "alignment" is not a concept that is particularly well understood. Rather than aligning the components of culture, skills, knowledge, structure, and strategy—the actual requirements for system alignment—we tend to focus almost exclusively on the component of "structure." As a noun, alignment refers to the degree of integration of an organization's core systems, structures, processes, and skills, as well as to the degree of connectedness of the people to the organization strategy. As a verb, alignment is a force like magnetism. It is what happens to scattered iron filings when you pass a magnet over them. Credibility of leadership influences alignment of people and organizational space activities.

CREDIBILITY OF LEADERSHIP

If people don't trust leadership, share the vision, or buy into the reason for the change, and if they are excluded from the planning process, there will be no successful change, regardless of how brilliant the strategy. Credibility is a foundation of leadership; if people don't believe in the messenger, they won't believe the message. With clarity, alignment, and credibility, organizational integrity grows.

INTEGRITY IN THE ORGANIZATION

Politics, resources, relationships, and structures flow in a complicated dance that is rarely predictable. Strong core values, flexibility, and adaptability are essential when working with an erratic environment. Success means encouraging diversity and different points of view. People need to know that their voice matters and feel permitted to state their opinions. This short statement from the "Partners in Leadership" blog says it all: "Organizational integrity is the term we use to describe the foundational value that is the engine behind getting things done. Three core values are foundational: Follow Through—do what you say you will do; Get Real—get to the truth; Speak Up—Say what needs to be said." [18]

ACCOUNTABILITY FOR PERFORMANCE

We often rush towards accountability without any foundation principles on which to base accountability. Clarity of purpose, alignment of effort, credibility in organization, and integrity of leadership set the table for implementation. These elements help form culture, the customs, traditions, and practices played out in day-to-day relationships. Ultimately, effective and transformative leadership is about sharing control and dispensing both accountability and authority throughout the organization, thus creating the conditions for organizational success.

The previously discussed Health Results Team created a mantra ..."we will boil the ocean one bucket at a time." We designed a game book that strategically built momentum by: creating dynamic tension inside the ministry and outside in the delivery system; using transparency and comparative reporting to search for truth and shift behaviour; using accountability as a disruptive catalyst; recognizing that the real value of any plan is process thinking, new conversations with new people to test old assumptions; and implementing tactics to engage a wide audience and win the day.

We developed velocity and delivered results by: recognizing time is the biggest enemy of change; protecting ourselves from too many competing demands; facing facts fearlessly; and capitalizing and leveraging momentum.

We nurtured selective collaborations with the right people by: acknowledging that the ministry could not deliver transformation by itself; engaging a new cadre of leaders; creating expert panels to shape policy and future directions; reporting on outcomes of expert panel work and acting on recommendations; and delivering on our promise. We asked questions to test assumptions held!

In changes that you have been involved in, was clarity of purpose clear? Did people ask what they were trying to win at in order to fulfill their purpose? Were leaders aware of the risks of misalignment? Did the size of the organization (number of employees, number of business lines, variety, and expectations) create complexity and challenges to alignment of effort?

What's your personal change mantra?

RENEWAL

We have all examined organizational documents that contain a moment of genuine insight and consensus—documents that defined a problem well and provided a clearly articulated innovative strategy. Unfortunately, these findings were never acted upon. Sadly, each document represents hours of volunteer and paid hours of hard work, often by the best and brightest individuals. Each document contained someone's ambition to make an impact, yet it was placed on a disregarded stack.

Leaders are expected to inspire others and to facilitate development of a shared vision through aligned corporate vision, goals, and principles. This expectation is achieved through planning, intuition, intention, practical skill set, relationship building, and keen business acumen. Successful leaders admit they do not have all the answers. Successful leaders are motivated to ask the right questions and are committed to self-development.

The following is an adaptation of an essay by Thompson and MacLeod titled "If We Had a Magic Wand". Let's imagine for a moment that we have been invited to a private/public-sector meeting. The focus is on one high-leverage play to humanize leadership. As we walk into the room filled with big-name leaders, our hearts begin to race. This is the who's who of leadership, and we have been given less than ten minutes to provide insights and advice.

We are struck by the way the stage for this discussion is set. The curtains are all drawn, blocking out the activity and reality happening outside. There is plenty of activity inside the room; the high-powered people in suits are talking among themselves. Stacks of leadership reports and studies surround them; including directives from top academic advisors who have been busy labouring away to create the best plan. We can overhear some of the conversations, like "time to get everyone on board";

and "maybe we should have invited customers, workers, managers, and emerging leaders here today so that they can hear our new humanizing leadership vision."

We know already that we have our work cut out for us. The leaders are proud; they believe they have seen the light, and they assume that when everyone follows their lead and jumps on board with the program, everything will be good in the public and private sector world.

Turning back to the gathering inside, we see people taking their seats. Formalities begin. The chairperson leads with, "Today, we are going to bring leadership to life. We are going to make it all happen with the help of leaders in this room. With all this intelligence around the table, we can determine the future. Once our vision is clear, we will email it to everyone!"

We are optimists, and rarely lost for words, but after this statement, we take an uncomfortable pause. While their intentions are honourable, their attitudes are archaic and paternalistic. The empowerment train left the station and most of these leaders were left standing. It used to take decades to move from an idea to mainstream; now it takes only a moment to ignite a movement. These changes redefine what it means to be a customer. It also fundamentally changes the way we need to work as employees. We step our message up a notch; we are in the midst of a profound shift—a Copernicus moment. People and relationships are the central force of an organization's ecosystem. When this new paradigm is embraced, the natural order of everything changes.

We pause and look at the leaders' faces. Some are with us, and others are clearly not. It's time to bring all of this into sharper focus and make the message more meaningful. We decide to walk over to the window and pull back the curtain. As the light shines through, we hope we have opened the hearts and minds in a vital few of these leaders. We want them to see not only the choices that need to be made, but also how the choices must be made differently than in the past. We think they realize they have to step out of the comfort of their own rooms and roles if change is going to occur. To help them see beyond the limits of their current perspective, we suggest walking outside, beyond the confines of the room, and experience being with those who are shaping the world right here, right now. We look out and see a friendly wave from the crowd.

Turning toward the group of leaders, we say: Ladies and gentlemen, the customers, workers, and managers will see us now. Are we ready for our own renewal?"[19]

Renewing yourself is an active process of your values and being. As discussed previously, it requires transformation above and below the neck. You can accomplish something in the right renewal direction every day in the micro interactions between you and the people you work with—in the empathy you demonstrate. Be realistic and optimistic ... and practice both!

Whenever I think about the topic of leadership and the future, I reflect on the multitude of individuals who graciously shared their time, words, wisdom, and encouragement with me along my leadership journey. Often, these individuals had confidence in me before I had confidence in my own ability. These individuals provided me with the essential space and pivotal opportunities to learn, experiment, fail, and grow.

My Top Ten Adaptive Action Learnings

1. While the management of change requires organizational form and capacity, too much structural reform, or acting too early, can allow bureaucratic instincts to calcify or freeze frame the ongoing reform.

2. Organizations don't change—people do or they don't. Transformation gets rocky not because of strategy but because the human dimension was not appreciated.

3. Large-scale change usually triggers emotional reactions: denial, negativity, choice, tentative acceptance, and commitment. Leadership can either facilitate this emotional process or ignore it at the peril of the transformation effort.

4. For today's sceptical employee audience, rhetoric without action quickly disintegrates into empty slogans and propaganda. What you do in the hallways is more powerful than what you say in the meeting room.

5. Misattribution, misinformation, and misinterpretation can be clarified when individuals talk directly to each other. An organization not only changes with different people, it changes with the same people when you converse about different topics. Shift from the power relationships to people relationships. Introduce new partners, beyond the traditional heavyweights, and by creating new forums for making decisions.

6. Keep evidence at the forefront. Generate useful and actionable information and refine it to produce good, measurable indicators. Create and publish narratives while waiting for the evidence to materialize. Do not leave a vacant space of "no information" open.

7. Trying to manage large-scale transformation with the same strategies used for incremental change is dangerous. Transformation is a re-definition of who we are and what we do. Past change success may be your greatest obstacle.

8. Course corrections are easier than trying to implement revolutionary reforms on a complete and comprehensive basis, especially through large bureaucratic organizations and over the objections of stakeholder organizations steeped in existing processes.

9. Accountability, transparency, and comparative reporting are very potent weapons in the service of truth, and in the face of resistance, whether from special interests, journalistic expose, isolated complaints, or even nostalgia.

10. Stay focused and clear about the destination, maintain momentum, and resist interesting detours. Pay attention to self-interest, single-issue lobbying, and expansion and entrenchment of rights-based discourse at the expense of a sense of responsibility.

To be a leader of change in this complex environment, one has to reconcile, and work with, ideas that are seemingly opposite of one another. Leaders find a "sweet spot" between the fundamentally paradoxical notions of the art and science of leadership. Having the personality, conceptual ability, artistic temperament, and practice of successful juxtaposition of opposites are key to successful leadership.

Renewal is brought on by a continual search and need for ways to further development. Leaders have a passion for learning and seek every opportunity to sustain personal development. Learning leaders accept that new skills, understanding, and knowledge are critical ingredients for personal and organizational success. Through learning, we extend our capacity to create—to be part of the generative process of life. Covey characterizes the principle of renewal as an upward spiral of continuous improvement for personal change. Individuals keep growing by learning, committing, and doing at increasingly higher levels, thus the metaphor of the spiral.

A leaders life is a series of trapeze bars that are seized and swung from progressively, grabbing the next bar just after as you let go of the previous. Between the bars is where you experience the most learning. It ends with a beautiful and inspiring sentiment: "…hurtling through the void, you just learn how to fly"[20]… and lead.

What are you learning between the trapeze bars?

MOVING FORWARD

For an organization to be optimized and reach its full potential, it must be adaptive to its environment. Success is dependent on the ability to manage the relationships within a particular system and the various environments that system interacts with. Consistent with complexity-science leadership theory, the basic premise is that adaptive leadership can apply to anyone, no matter where they are located in the 'organizational human system' or their level within the hierarchy. An attempt is made to demonstrate the image of human systems within human systems and the interdependencies and influences they have on each other. For the team leader, the system could be their immediate task environment, whereas the extended system might be the organization as a whole. For a CEO and executive team, their immediate environment could be the organization as a whole, whereas the extended system could encompass the external task environment.

It is time to think about organizations as living systems with the capacity to self-organize, sustain themselves, and move toward greater complexity. We often hear people say they want their organization to be adaptive, flexible, self-renewing, resilient, and ever learning. This sounds like a living system, yet many leaders only know how to lead and manage an organization as if it were a machine. It is hard to accept what we do not know, do not control, and do not want to learn. The awakening of these truths demands a shift in how we manage and lead. All the things that have been traditionally labelled as intangibles will become important and visible.

It matters a great deal whether leaders conceive of their organizations as being like machines or like living, adaptive systems. It matters because it shapes the roles they and their people play. It matters because it bears directly on their ability to tap human potential. It matters because the times have changed, and mechanically based leadership and organizational practices are not adequate to the adaptive challenges being faced.

Let's Imagine a Future With...

1. *Improved relationships*, in particular how trust, and leadership that models trust and relationship-building responsibility, can be enhanced.

2. *Much more conversation* among leaders at policy, management, and practice levels, to develop shared language and logic, and to sort out who needs to do what in the organizational white space.

3. *Identity focus,* especially amplifying focus on what is in this for *us*, not just me.

4. *Optimal management for the optimal flow* of accurate information that, like the air we breathe, strengthens connections among people and assists us to transform data into meaningful knowledge.

5. *Structured opportunities and incentives* for teams to reflect on the feedback loops provided by this information in a shared learning network for continuous improvement.

6. *Leaders taking advantage of the unused skills, talents, and potentialities of everyone* in the organization and overcoming the intellectual, emotional, and systemic barriers in the way of creating a truly healthy, learning organization.

REFLECTIONS AND CONSIDERATIONS

What's the level of your organizational complacency? Are you ready to reframe the conversation and narrative from "what is the matter?" to "what matters to you?"

Where is the creative tension in your organization? Are your leadership actions creating innovation or fear and anxiety?

What are you doing to encourage formal and informal leaders at all levels in your organization to hammer out meaningful questions?

Ultimately, effective leadership is about sharing control and dispersing both accountability and authority throughout organizations and systems, thus creating the enabling conditions for leadership to be transformative. How are you engaging others in developing your change-reform-transformation purpose and enabling others to see the part they play in achieving that purpose?

Are you choosing your frustrations? What is frustrating or motivating you most as a leader? What does it take to work with the team you have? How can you commit to helping them succeed?

Questions need to be asked to focus leaders on accountability, self-reflection, honesty, and purpose. Which questions? Here are eight questions to get you started: What do you want to create and contribute to the system, as an individual, team, and an organization? What is your vision of achievement? What does achievement look like? What will it take from you to do it?

What are you doing right now to reach your vision? What is hampering you? What are you afraid of losing? What might you gain by doing something differently?

Do you agree with this statement? "There isn't anything as stable and predictable as an organization full of fixers on the hunt for fixes. Judging that the world is outside, distinct and separate from us, is a simple human reflex. We are wired that way. Instead of automatically focusing on the outside, turn around and focus inside." [21]

CHAPTER VI
CHOOSE NOT TO MIMIC LEADERSHIP PERSONAS

"When it all boils down, it's about embracing each others' stories and just maybe finding the synergy to collaborate for common good."
~D. Jones

INTRODUCTION

From the book Introduction through to Chapter V, I invited you to embark on a learning journey with your own personal perspectives and reasons for turning the pages. How this book impacts you and your leadership journey is not revealed, but I sincerely hope the leadership insights provided have broadened your personal understanding and instilled enthusiasm for the limitless possibilities that surround you.

In Chapters I through III, I discussed the personal and human side of leadership. This mindset recognizes that people have something to contribute and should be treated with dignity and respect. I asked questions about reflection and our obsession with doing and achieving, which often diminishes our ability to focus on ourselves, who we are, and our strengths. I discussed the changing nature of work and how it is having a huge impact on our most important asset, our people. This has major implications for leadership. These changes result in a re-invent of relationships to leverage uniquely human skills: empathy, social and emotional intelligence.

In Chapters IV and V, I discussed the fact that as the organizational environment becomes more complex and ambiguous, there is even a greater need to humanize leadership. Yet many organizations continue to position leadership as a top down instrument. Linear walls that created and delineated competitors, governments and technologies into discreet boxes are crumbling in front of our eyes. I discussed existing mindsets, and the paradox of simultaneous continuity and change.

Reflection, people matter, and healthy relationships create a new and deeper meaning of purpose, using a mindful mindset that is capable of balancing the ongoing and relentless pushes and pulls on the human organizational system.

In Chapter VI, I encourage you to blossom the natural leader within you. I follow this up with a future look at leadership challenges. I close with a personal note about my journey.

BLOSSOM THE LEADER WITHIN

Our quest for knowledge stems from our innate curiosity. Our minds are filled with infinite questions pertaining to life and all it encompasses. Many of us are reluctant to accept any one idea, experience, or belief as a static conclusion. We believe there is room for discovery and personal growth, and that life is a series of unturned stones.

Learning is not an end, in and of itself, but rather a means to process our experiences, tune our versatility, and establish the necessary skills for life's constant shifts. Leadership knowledge, like all knowledge, is not limited or bound. Leadership knowledge demands perpetual growth and adaptation. The obstacles we face within ourselves, and the organizations we serve, must continually be outgrown.

Learning requires us to be vulnerable and open to varying perspectives, and to test the validity of our beliefs and those held by others. Learning starts with our involvement, questioning, and curiosity, followed by self-reflection. Few learning's are isolated or self-contained; most travel through our knowledge and experience bank, and alter our assumptions and beliefs. Self-reflection enables the digestion of new learning's.

If learning cannot be imposed, why do we attempt to change the people we are positioned to lead? We attempt to rewire people, and people systems, as though they were robots. A human system requires much more than a simple reboot or upgrade.

There are no organizational initiatives, no "flavour of the year" training, telling, explaining, coercing, or convincing that can allow you to learn anything from anyone else. You have to make that choice yourself. The choices and challenges you face, as a leader will be constant; how you prepare and equip yourself to manage your leadership will determine your path.

Ancient Zen wisdom asserts, "The body of leadership has four limbs: enlightenment and virtue; speech and action; humaneness and justice; etiquette and law. Enlightenment and virtue are the root of the teaching; humaneness and justice are the branches of the teaching. With no root, it is impossible to stand; with no branches it is impossible to be complete. The honour of the community is not for the leader. The plenitude of the necessities of life is not for the follower students. All of it is for the way of enlightenment. Therefore, a good leader should honour first enlightenment and virtue, and be careful in speech and action. To be able to be a student, one should think first of goodness and right, and follow etiquette and law. Thus, the leadership cannot stand without the followers, and the followers cannot develop without the leadership. The leadership and the followers are like the body and the arms, like the head and the feet. Therefore, it is said, followers keep the communities, and the communities keep virtue. If the leadership has no virtue, the community is on the verge of decline." [1]

Leadership is about inspiring people and teams to do their best and enabling questioning and decision-making at every level of the organization. "The root of the word inspires means to breathe in, to fill with spirit. Inspiration is the capacity to move people by reaching in and filling them with a deeper source of meaning." [2]

It is about recognizing and valuing the contributions of others and demonstrating astute confidence and trust in the ability of individuals and teams to coordinate and control their work. Core requisites for leadership include the following qualities: operating from genuine and honourable personal values, principles, and ethics; shaping and maintaining corporate culture; responding to and managing within dynamic circumstances and contexts; having a clear personal purpose and inspiring a shared vision with others; having healthy relationships that result in integrity of character; leading with conviction and courage; and illustrating commitment to learning and renewal.

Like it or not, you already have a leadership reputation. You have a reputation based on how you get things done and how you interact with others. To leverage your leadership or to steer it in a different direction, you need to get a clear picture of how others perceive you today. Take control. You're in charge of your leadership, so invest in your learning, and development as a leader.

As Warren Bennis suggests "To become a leader, you must become yourself, become the maker of your life. Know thyself, then, means separating who you are and who you want to be from what the world thinks your are and wants you to be. Until you make you life your own, you're walking around in borrowed clothes." [3]

Think about it. Why are you a leader? Are you ever really prepared? Why should people follow you? Start by paying attention to how you work, not just what you know or what you accomplish. How do you learn? How do you share information, make decisions, and influence others? How do you build and nurture relationships? Just by paying attention to these questions, you'll gain insight.

FUTURE FOCUSSED LEADERSHIP

There is an abundance of brilliant minds, brave souls, compassionate hearts, technological wizards, and creative geniuses amongst us. The mechanism for change is already present. Human beings are meaning makers. Purpose, empathy, and shared meaning are critical as they built the foundations for stability and growth. The behaviours and relationships of the players must be harnessed, and a proper direction must be determined. The vital realization that people and relationships bind organizations must continue to advance to the forefront. Stale protocols, outmoded agendas, incomplete strategies, forceful top-down mandates, self-serving ambitions, and unavailing quick fixes must be abandoned. I have witnessed these insertions for a number of decades, and they fail to work.

We need to stop the never-ending meetings of talk with no action or follow up. We need to stop the never-ending dance that has executives pirouetting around managers, and the never-ending dance of management and front-line workers twirling around customer needs. We must stop our territorial divides and self-absorbed behaviours and mindsets. When will we progress beyond hesitancy and embrace action? Silence, unawareness, indifference, and complacency are enemies of organizational improvement and sustainability.

Yes, there are a myriad of storms brewing. For example, there is a financial storm that is dashing against revenues: an online shopping storm coupled with a social media storm changing consumer behaviours, and a worker storm that is taking on greater responsibility for finding the solutions for the lack of system alignment. Regardless of the impending storms, this is an exciting time to be a leader, as we listen to and observe the many storms that are gathering. Although we use the term "system," we need to ask if we have a system of services designed to work in unison to create an intentional outcome. Interaction brings growth, change, commitment, and values shared. For an organization, or a network/system of organizations, to be successful, each of its interdependent parts must be designed to operate in sync with one another. A smoothly operating system is not produced by a series of isolated actions. Cohesion stems from an orchestration of interactions at the right time, for the right person, in the right places.

Conventional tweaks and Band-Aid approaches only prolong the ills of human organizational systems. The perpetuation of the status quo must be terminated. Leaders need to be gritty; they need to stand up against outdated systems and relationship patterns. They need to use their voice, influence, and energy to break down and remove each and every component that obstructs system change. Leaders must strip the system of its futility and detritus so the system can become nimble and capable of transformation.

Leadership is hard and adaptive work. Leadership is dynamic; it morphs, and moulds to circumstance and is action-oriented. Leadership is neither a demand for power nor acquiescence to the demand. Leadership is the experience arising from combining two motivations. First, you create community through a commitment for relationship building based on an important cause or principle. Second, you organize resources to reach an endgame.

Chasing the latest leadership fad is easy/lazy work. Big change is messy and will not follow a tidy, linear, and predictable fashion. Identifying and changing behaviours across a large and complex local, regional, provincial, or national organization is a significant challenge. The biggest challenge is sustaining efforts over time. Ultimately, effective leadership is about sharing control and dispersing both accountability and authority throughout organizations, thus creating enabling conditions for organizational leadership to be transformative.

It is up to future leaders to lead with integrity, to model the values and purpose of the organization in every aspect of their work, and to encourage such behaviour at all levels of the organization. In order to survive and thrive in this new environment, leaders must respond to this prevailing sentiment while continuing to focus on the purpose and reasons they became leaders in the first place. The policies and procedures of an organization can end up constraining people from getting their work done. There are also significant trade offs in organizations between goals, such as cheaper, faster, better. It is impossible to obtain all three. Each moment is a reconstruction of the past in the present, accompanied by simultaneous continuity and change in the present. The future is continually under construction, and it is unknown and unpredictable.

Every day, we witness how the global Internet of public opinion drives the need to address the immediate problem quickly, but often that doesn't actually produce an evidence-informed, effective solution. Often the public discourse tends to narrow our view of societal problems. With that, we are now seeing a growth in self-interest, single-issue lobbying, and expansion and entrenchment of rights-based discourse, at the expense of a sense of responsibility. Policy challenges are viewed as bipolar, with false dichotomies narrowing the field of policy options. Often, this creates a leadership mindset that includes: "let's keep our heads down"; "now is not the time to be out front"; "let others go first and we'll see what happens"; "this too shall pass"; and "let's just wait it out."

In many settings we hear "hurry up"; "go fast"; "stop." Leaders, eager to please, respond accordingly by taking the problem on their own shoulders and developing solutions that might alleviate a symptom, but not the underlying problem. A major pitfall of leadership is assuming that you're the one who must come up with the answers instead of developing adaptive capacity—the capacity of people—to face root-cause problems and take responsibility for them. Change requires more than identifying the problem and then offering a call to action. It requires looking beyond the problem and finding the source of trouble.

B. Johansen, in *"Leaders Make the Future,"* offers a thesis of four overlapping future forecasts: the challenge of volatility, uncertainty, complexity, and ambiguity (Vuca). Vuca conjures up an image in which disruption is the new normal and leaders need to learn new skills in order to manage within this future.

Let's Imagine Leaders Making the Future With...

1. *The Maker Instinct*: The ability to exploit their inner drive to build and grow things, as well as connect with others in the making.

2. *Clarity:* The ability to see through messes and contradictions to a future that others cannot yet see and communicate with clarity in confusing times.

3. *Dilemma Flips:* The ability to turn dilemmas into advantages and opportunities.

4. *Immediate Learning:* The ability to immerse themselves in unfamiliar environments and to learn from them in a first-person way.

5. *Bio-Empathy*: The ability to see organizations as living systems—to understand, reflect, and learn from its patterns.

6. *Constructive Depolarization*: The ability to calm tense situations and bring people from divergent cultures towards positive engagement.

7. *Quiet Transparency*: The ability to be open and authentic about what matters without being overly self-promoting.

8. *Rapid Prototyping*: The ability to create quick, early versions of innovation with expectations that later success will require early results.

9. *Smart-Mob Organizing*: The ability to create, engage, and nurture purposeful social networks through intelligent use of electronic and other media.

10. *Common Creation*: The ability to seed, nurture, and grow shared assets that can benefit all and allow competition at a higher level.[4]

Private and public businesses face a virtually unprecedented variety of challenges, from harvesting profits in mature economies with flat or declining growth, to establishing toeholds in emerging countries, to creating the next wave of disruptive innovation, to working through the complexity of changing regulation, and everything in between.

Each of these unique challenges requires a unique kind of humanizing leader. One size does not fit all.

MY PERSONAL JOURNEY
AND TRUTHS

As mentioned in the Introduction, I have been working on this book throughout my personal and professional life. On my personal leadership journey, these are some of the personal truths I have come to believe and cherish.

Leadership does not come with, nor should ever have, a how-to manual. My personal approach to leadership is not extracted from a store or library shelf, but rather is a construct developed over time. All the leadership books and articles, including this book, should not be taken as a recipe for leadership; instead they should be viewed as instruments to create internal dialogue and raise questions.

Every leader is unique, for we all stem from our own circumstance. I chose not to mirror or mimic leadership personas, and instead opted to blossom the leader within me. My passion for this idea started early. As a young boy, my job in the family was to bring peace at times of great tension. I learned how to listen, see around the obvious, interpret, and take risks to de-escalate potential explosive situations. In the process, I took personal responsibility to shape and define my personal persona and way of being. Lucky for me, my mother and grandfather were present to provide support, to build me up, and to honour the role I was playing in our complicated home environment.

At seventy-one years of age, I see how my early experiences organized my entire personal and professional life, and after years studying, living, and breathing leadership, I still continue to evolve as a leader. Every new experience presents an opportunity to reflect, adjust, and grow. I have an extensive past to look back on and assess. I know the pressures that can hamper genuine leadership, such as career promotion, politics, short-term gain, and stubbornness. I have also been granted many years to get to understand myself better.

As previously discussed in Chapter I, creating my personal and "living" definition of leadership affected how I thought about my roles, choices made, how I acted, my relationship with others, and ultimately, personal and organizational results. As I began to immerse myself in the narrative of my personal leadership definition, I found myself questioning and challenging my perspective on long-held beliefs and views. A transformation occurred as I reflected, and it moved me to reframe my own thinking. Reflective replies to my personal leadership questions came from a compassionate, experience-based perspective of what is needed to achieve organizational dynamic wholeness: cohesiveness; flexibility; interconnectedness; cost-effectiveness; values; and the commitment of people above all else.

At times, my leadership journey was like living on a three-dimensional chessboard. On one level, multiple product line and business units, a diverse workforce, and networks. On another level, shifting customer demands, sustainability issues, regulator systems, and geopolitics. On the last level, there's financial performance, the twenty-four-hour demands of the Internet, and the menacing self-interested parties. There's also one further complexity to the three-dimensional chessboard: Do we know if we are playing the right pieces at the right time, and did we set the right table before dining? This may be the truth behind the saying "the stronger you become, the more life challenges."

I eventually began to realize the most important tools I had are the natural tools I had gained through experience, learning, and mentoring. This was confirmed during a graduate-studies course on system thinking and complexity. Halfway through the lecture, a wave of personal validation hit me. I remember saying to myself, "I do this stuff! I have been doing it for years. I just didn't know about the science behind it." With a new understanding of the science, I kept growing by learning, committing, and doing at increasingly higher levels, thus the metaphor of the learning spiral.

To ensure my personal values and goals matched the vision, culture, and direction of the organization, my human hard drive and personal-value maps got tested continuously. Deep down, no matter what leadership position we occupy in a group or a team or an organization, sooner or later we are all going to be put to the test. Over time, when tested, I moved beyond my complacencies, embraced the current realities, and believed in my abilities to lead. In order to align these elements, I needed to go inward and spend sufficient time in reflection to be alone with my thoughts, anxieties, and quiet victories, and assess myself in order to bring forth placidity and composure to cope with the brutal realities I faced. It's only as you examine your life that you are able to identify the changes you need to make in order to develop your leadership.

For my leadership development, the three overlapping threads communicated in this book, "reflection fuels," "people matter," and "relationships make the difference," were and continue to be my leadership foundation blocks. The extent to which I embraced or enhanced these understandings impacted my leadership abilities. Did I always find the right balance of the three threads? Did I fully appreciate how and when the three overlapping threads where in play, as well as my contributions to the play? Short answer? No! My capacity to manage organizational complexities, paradoxes, and pressures was indicative of how well I incorporated the three threads into my leadership approach. Leadership growth and excellence is not a linear path; it is the accumulation of setbacks, discovery, perseverance, and letting go. My leadership was learned through trial and error, through mucking up, and having the gumption to learn. Without this experience, I would have run the risk of becoming a leadership theorist versus a leader.

I am human. I made mistakes and continue to make mistakes. The difference between the past and present is that I no longer allow my pride or ego to get in the way of learning from mistakes. In fact, I am no longer afraid to make mistakes. I take ownership of all the shortcomings and advances I am responsible for. I am comfortable in my leadership role and with my leadership competencies. I do not cast blame or use others as scapegoats. The day I admitted to myself that I was not perfect, and that I was good in spots, was the day I became liberated. I no longer played the imposter game. My leadership liberation-growth demanded that I should release my ego, understand my limitations, acknowledge my weaknesses, and possess a hunger for personal progress.

Letting go and becoming the leader within allowed me to see that my leadership vision was often constrained by my personal shackles: my ego, the facade of being "all knowing," the avoidance of my vulnerabilities, ignoring my limitations, and failing to utilize the aid and greatness of those around me. An organization is much more than any one particular individual. Through experiences, I learned firsthand that the more you let go, the stronger you become. Very simply, leadership is about looking within and all around you. We must lead and inspire by example, by personifying the qualities of honesty, integrity, resilience, and confidence, demonstrating how leadership, too, is a process of self-development, not an ultimate arrival. Leadership starts with, and is elevated by, a solid relationship with self.

Letting go reduced my rigidity and narrow sightedness, allowed me to stay flexible, present, and engaged with the activities, understandings, and insights from every facet of the organization. I learned the importance of being there to serve and becoming one with the organization. I worked hard to resist the temptation to wear the official organizational title as a badge to signify "I am the leader." Instead, I chose a path of earning the respect and trust of those I worked with. The pretense that I, as a leader, was above the whole, or superior to them, began to wash away.

Saying "I don't know" and reaching out to others who had skills I did not possess made me a stronger and better leader. My need to impress has been eradicated. Perhaps it was easier for me to come to these understandings as I near the closing of my leadership career. I can only imagine how my trajectory and impact may have differed if I had come to these understandings earlier in my career when I competed with others for advancement, for recognition, for power. Letting go and accepting the leadership gift I had and did not have was not for discussion or personal and honest reflection.

That said, leadership is not a race; I believe I learned the lessons I needed and grew into my being as intended. When we have some distance between the immediate, and have the time to reflect on the past, it is easy to view the components that influence our being—components that are often outside our periphery by choice, due to the leadership persona we attempt to uphold. An authentic leadership approach that is reflective of the people, experiences, opportunities, risks, reflections, and personal understandings is what collectively sculpts our personal leadership journey. Again, no amount of leadership theory or talk could influence me as strongly as being thrown into the ring.

The expression 'it takes a community to raise a child' is also true for leadership development. My career has been built upon decisions made, opportunities given, and the collaboration of the teams I was fortunate enough to be a part of. I was lucky, in that I had a believer and supporter in my corner every step of the way. Every leadership opportunity presented, whether that meant a move to a new position, organization, city, or province was discussed with my life-long partner and best friend, Linda. Over time, I began to realize that she had become my trusted executive coach. She created a safe and personal vessel that nurtured and helped me sustain my leadership development

The overall condition and potential of a substantial and sustainable vessel is dependent upon an entire crew. No matter the will or knowhow, reaching the chosen destination is highly uncertain. Whereas the potential and effectiveness of the vessel is fully realized when the crew work in unison—when the collective is working together to reach the intended destination, zigzagging as necessary when unpredictable elements are thrown at them, the prowess and skillset of each member drastically increases the probability of reaching the new destination.

I owe an equal amount of recognition to the organizations and people I have worked with; the leaders that made a lasting impact on my life are those who revealed their underbelly. They were unafraid to show who they were. This included faults and strengths. They made no apologies. Organizationally speaking, they placed as much emphasis on those around them as they did on themselves. They made the people around them better by providing opportunity and believing in their ability. I can only hope for the same kind of impact. Leadership is not about the roles and titles we hold but the impact we make on our organizations as a whole. In my opinion, to bring the very best out of an organization, you have to bring the very best out of the people, maximize and nurture the relationships that are connected within it, and keep yourself in check by reflecting upon your actions and values.

Over my career, I have had many teachable moments, and one in particular stands out for me, reading to my grandchildren. Recently I read to my youngest grandson my favourite book on leadership, *The Little Engine That Could,* the children's classic. It's about a journey, community involvement, overcoming road blocks, crisis conquering, competition, ego, and self-indulgence, work jurisdiction and turf, old versus new technology, courage, and the power within, and getting on with it. The key leadership message is simple; saying and believing at a deep level "I Think I Can, I Think I Can" in an organization that sets the tracks up the hill and at the right angle of challenge. The story reinforced for me the three threads in the book: "reflection fuels"; "people matter"; and "relationships make the difference."

Writing Chapter VI fills me with all kinds of emotions. My leadership journey has been a ride, and I am a fortunate guy! I am so impressed by the calibre of people that I have had the privilege to work with. I had a front-row seat for incredible leadership learning experiences. What started off as a writing and communications task turned into a journey of self-reflection, as demonstrated by the evolution of the comments found throughout the book. I am a lifelong student of leadership-and-change management. I have learned that a leader must frequently return to a critical question: Why is it important to adapt and change?

Given that leadership is personal, I made a deliberate decision not to give direction. As you delved into the pages, a familiar voice was consistently whispering, guiding, and challenging self-reflection. The book offers a candid "balcony view" of issues confronting leaders. The book suggests options and provides information. It stimulates personal reflection and self-acceptance, to cultivate and enhance personal leadership gifts, and to unfold the knowledge from within. It achieves this by interpreting the potential for interconnection between how reflection fuels, people matter, and relationships make the difference. It speaks through the art and science of leadership to enable the forces of humanizing leadership to grow and flow. The bottom line is that what goes on between people defines what an organization is and what it can become.

The Chinese philosopher Lao Tao said, "When I let go of what I am, I become what I might be."[5] Letting go creates the space for relationships and a collective identity to develop, for information to be shared, and for the talents of everyone within human organizational systems to be valued. On the strength of these behavioural and mindset shifts, we can achieve the collective accountability required for making organizational improvements. It's about choice.

Every road and intersection I chose presented a choice, and following a road never travelled before was a journey. On my personal leadership-learning journey, there were long and short roads, smooth and rocky roads, crooked and straight paths. I hope my personal leadership map stays open, connectable in all its dimensions, and capable of being dismantled or modified. What I see depends on what I am prepared to see. Given that I am still heavily engaged in this conversation, I believe reflection fuels, people matter, and relationships make the difference. Do you?

Are you "Humanizing Your Leadership"?

If you want to continue this conversation, please visit my new "Cultivate Your Leadership Blog" at www.cultivateyourleadership.com

"It is not the truth that we do not know that does us in, but the truths we know and don't practice."
~Mark Twain

References

Chapter I – What Most Leadership Conversations Gloss Over

1. Drucker, P. "Managing Knowledge Means Managing Oneself." Drucker Foundation Letter Essay, 2000.

2. Aristotle Quote. *Brainy Quotes.*

3. Bergen, P. "Why So Many Leadership Programs Ultimately Fail." Harvard Business Review, 2013

4. Ledoux, L. "Synthesis of the Practice of Adaptive Leadership." Internet, 2009.

5. Ramos, I. "The Organizational Mind." Portugal: University of Minho, 2006.

6. Senge, P. "Systems Citizenship: The Leadership Mandate for this Millennium." *Future Leader Blog*, 2006.

7. Hill, A. A Review of J. Pfeffer's New Book *Leadership BS. Financial Times*, 2015.

8. Mintzberg, H. "Capital 'L' Versus Small 'L' Leadership." CBC Radio Interview, 1999.

9. Kouzes, J. Posner, B. *"The Leadership Challenge."* San Francisco: Jossey-Bass, 2012.

10. Kotter, J., Matsushita. *Leadership: Lessons from the 20th Century's Most Remarkable Entrepreneur.* Free Press, 1997.

11. Benson, D. "How To Determine Your Personal Leadership Philosophy." American Association For Physician Leadership News, 2018

12. Jay, J., *"The Inner Edge: The 10 Practices of Personal Leadership."* Praeger, 2009

13. Bennis, W. *On Becoming a Leader.* Perseus Publishing, 1989.

14. Dickson, G. Tholl, B. *"Bringing Leadership to Life in Health."* Springer, 2014.

15. Menon T., L. Thompson. "Putting a Price on People Problems at Work." *Harvard Business Review*, 2016.

16. Holmberg, C. "The Most Dangerous Leadership Traps And A Daily Practice That Will Save You." Fast Company News, October 08, 2016.

17. Short R. "Learning in Relationship. Learning in Action Technologies." Bellevue Washington, 1998.

18. James W. "Internet." *Encyclopedia of Philosophy.*

19. Einstein, A. *Brainy Quotes.*

20. Taylor, M., H. MacLeod. "Bridging the Leadership Gap." Essay. Longwoods Publishing, 2015.

21. Scharmer, O. *Theory U: Learning from the Future as it Emerges.* Berrett-Koehler Publishers, 2009.

22. Collins, J. *Good to Great: Why Some Companies Make the Leap and Others Don't.* Harper Collins Publishers, 2001.

23. Barrett, R. *The New Leadership Paradigm.* Rutledge, 2010.

24. Goleman, D. *Primal Leadership: Unleashing the Power of Emotional Intelligence.* Harvard Business Press, 2013.

25. Daskal, L. "Are You Lying to Yourself About Your Leadership?" (blog) 2016.

26. Oshry, B. *Seeing Systems.* Berrett-Keohler Publishers, 2007.

27. McLuhan, M. *Understanding the Media – The Extension of Man,* 1964.

28. Maletz, M., N. Nohria. "Managing Within White Space." Harvard Business Review, 2001.

29. Dickson, G. "Leaders in Action – Leaders in Inaction: The Change Dilemma." Longwoods Publishing Open Letters Series on Leadership and Change, 2017.

30. Rucco, A. "What I learned From My Personal Board Of Directors." Longwoods Publishing Open Letter Series on Leadership and Change, 2017.

31. "Story of Lao-Tzu." *Shen Yun Performing Arts Blog,* 2013.

32. Arthur, W.B. *Sense Making in the New Economy.* Xerox PARC, Palto Alto, 1999.

33. Crossman, M., G. Seijts, and J. Gandz. *Developing Leadership Character.* Routledge Publishing, 2015

Chapter II – Are Hearts, Spirits and Minds Important to You?

1. Branson, R. www.Goodreads.com/7356284

2. Sokolow, S. "Integrating Mind Body and Spirit." Centre for Empowerment Website Post, 2013.

3. "Kronos Study. The Employee Burnout Crisis," 2017.

4. Truven Health Analytics. "Hospital Employees Are Less Healthy and More Likely to Be Hospitalized More Than General Public," 2010.

5. Menon, T., L. Thompson. "Putting a Price on People Problems at Work." *Harvard Business Review*, 2016.

6. CCP Inc. (Myers Griggs) and Thomas-Kilmann, "Study on Work Place Conflict," 2009.

7. Parliament of Australia. Committee on Work Place Bullying, 2010.

8. Phillips, J. "Workplace Violence Against Healthcare Workers in USA." The *New England Journal of Medicine*, 2016.

9. Smith, S. "Presenteeism Cost Business 10 Times More Than Absenteeism." *EHS Today*, 2016.

10. "Presenteeism: At Work—But Out of It." Harvard Business Review

11. Dickson, G., Tholl, B. *"Bringing Leadership to Life In Health."* Springer, 2014.

12. Adeco Staffing Study, on USA Workforcve Skills, 2008

13. Hay Group Report on Soft Skills, 2014

14. Deloitte Report on Global Human Capital Trends, 2015.

15. Burch, N. "Learning Stages Model." Gordon Training International Website, 2015.

16. Entel, T., S. Grayson. "The Empathy Engine: Turning Customer Service into a Sustainable Advantage." Booz&Co, 2007.

17. Paper – "Unleashing the Potential of Pride Builders." Booz&Co, 2007.

18. Hesket et al. "The Service Profit Chain." *Harvard Business Review*; 1994.

19. Abraham Lincoln Quote. *Brainy Quotes.*

20. Covey, S. *Seven Habits of Highly Successful People*, 1984.

21. Greenleaf, R. *Power of Servant Leadership.* Berrett-Koehler Publishers, 1998.

22. Coelho, P. Official Website, 2007.

23. Hayles, R., A. Russell. *The Diversity Directive.* Irvin Publishing, 1997.

24. Kouzes, J., Posner, B. *"The Leadership Challenge."* San Francisco: Jossey-Bass, 2012.

25. Parr. S. "Culture Eats Strategy For Lunch." Fast Company, January 24, 2012.

26. Ledoux, L. "Synthesis of the Practice of Adaptive Leadership." Internet, 2009.

27. Short, R. "Learning in Relationships." Learning in Action Technologies Inc. Bellevue Washington, 1998.

Chapter III - Organizational Elasticity and Effectiveness

1. Short, R. "Learning in Relationship." Learning in Action Technologies Inc. Bellevue Washington, 1998.

2. Ditton, M., H. MacLeod. "Health System Relationships: A Paradigm Shift." Essay. Longwoods Publishing, 2014.

3. Scharmer, O. Lecture. Massachusetts Institute of Technology, 2001.

4. MacLeod, H. "A Last Word from the Balcony of Personal Reflection." Essay. Longwoods Publishing, 2015.

5. Dykstra, J. "Intent and Leadership Action." (blog), 2011.

6. Thor O. "The Heart of Leadership." (blog) 2013.

7. Mckinsey & Company. "Why Leadership Development Programs Fail," 2014.

8. Wolf story found online.

9. Daskal, L. *Leadership Blog*. 2016.

10. Axelrod, R., H. MacLeod. "Engaging the Staff," Health Forum Journal, 45 (3), 2003.

11. MacLeod, H., R. Alvarez. "Four Mindset Shifts: Relationships, Identity, Information and People Potential."Essay. Longwoods Publishing, 2013.

12. Axelrod, R. *Terms of Engagement. Second Edition.* Berrett-Koehler Publishers Inc., 2010.

Chapter IV – Paradox of Simultaneous Continuity and Change

1. Meuser E., H. MacLeod. "Lessons from the Stanley Cup Playoffs." Essay. Longwoods Publishing, 2013.

2. MacLeod, H., G. Dickson. "Healthcare Leadership Contradictions." Longwoods Publishing, 2015.

3. MacLeod, H., D. Cochrane. "Danger of Simplicity." Essay. Longwoods Publishing, 2013.

4. Zimmerman, B., S. Globerman. "Complicated and Complex Systems." Commission on the Future of Healthcare in Canada, 2004.

5. MacLeod, H. "Where We Live, How We Live, How We Make A Living." Essay. Long-woods Publishing. 2015.

6. Short, R. "Learning in Relationship." Learning in Action Technologies Inc. Bellevue Washington, 1998.

7. Plsek, P. "Redesigning health care with insights from the science of complex adaptive systems." Institute of Medicine, Crossing the Quality Chasm. The National Academies Press, 2001.

8. Lindstrom, R., H. MacLeod. "Getting a Grip on Complexity." Essay. Longwoods Publishing, 2015.

9. Marion, R., M. Uhl-Bien. "Leadership in Complex Organizations." *Leadership Quarterly* (12), 2001.

10. Capra, F. *The Hidden Connections: A Science for Sustainable Living.* Anchor Books, 2002.

11. Senge, P. *The Fifth Discipline.* Doubleday Currency, 1990.

12. Ghandi, M. *Brainy Quotes.*

13. Ledoux, L. "Synthesis of the Practice of Adaptive Leadership." Internet, 2009.

14. Scharmer, O., K. Kaufer. *Leading from The Emerging Future.* Berrett-Koehler, 2007.

15. *Educause Blog.* "Asking Question Can Help You Become A Better Leader." 2017.

16. Gowen, B., H. MacLeod. "Caring, Coping and Crying." Essay. Longwoods Publishing, 2014.

17. Drucker, P. *Managing in the Next Society.* New York, New York: St. Martin's Griffin. 2002

18. Revell, T., Goolge. "Deep Mind NHS Data." *New Science Magazine,* May 2017.

19. Posner, B., J. Kouzes. *The Truth About Leadership.* Jossey-Bass, 2010.

20. Pollard, D. "System Thinking and Complexity 101." World Blog, June 08, 2014.

Chapter V - Adaptive Action and Leadership

1. Marcus, A. *Big Winners and Big Losers.* FT Press, 2005.

2. Jung, C. *Memories Dreams Reflection.* Vintage Books.

3. Lego Museum Exhibit, Billund Denmark.

4. Senge, P. "System Citizenship - Leadership Mandate for this Millennium." Speech, 2006.

5. Ledoux, L. "Synthesis of the Practice of Adaptive Leadership." Internet, 2009

6. Heifetz, R. "Adaptive Learning." *Healthcare Journal.* Vol. 38, No. 4, 1995.

7. Fenn M. "Reinvigorating Publicly Funded Medicare in Ontario." Canadian Public Administration Journal. Vol 49. 4. 2006.

8. Stacey, R., D. Griffin, and P. Shaw. *Complexity and Management: Fad or Radical Challenge to System Thinking.* Routledge, 2000.

9. Meuser E., H. MacLeod. "Lessons from the Stanley Cup Playoffs." Essay. Longwoods Publishing, 2013.

10. Shep, S., K. Cardiff, and H. MacLeod. "Resiliency – Time for A Change." Longwoods Publishing, 2014.

11. Petrie, N. *Wake Up!* Center for Creative Leadership White Paper, 2014

12. Csikszentmihalyi, M. *Flow: The Psychology of Optimal Experience.* New York: Harper & Row, 1990.

13. Cabane, O. F. (2012). *The Charisma Myth: How Anyone Can Master the Art and Science of Personal Magnetism.* New York: Portfolio/ Penguin.

14. Dowd, M. (June 1, 2013). "She's Getting Her Boots Dirty." *New York Times.* Web

15. Heifetz, R. "Leadership Without Easy Answers." *Harvard University Press*, 1994.

16. Finegood D., H. MacLeod. "Blurring the Lines Between Research, Evaluation and Outcome." Essay. Longwoods Publishing, 2015.

17. Fritz, R. "Path of Least Resistance." Website/home page, 2007.

18. The Accountability Training & Cultural Change Company. "Partners in Leadership Blog", 2016

19. Thompson L., H. MacLeod. "If We Had a Magic Wand" Essay. Longwoods Publishing, 2014

20. Parry, D. *"Warriors of the Heart."* BookSurge Publishing, 2009.

21. Short, R. "Learning in Relationship." Learning in Action Technologies Inc. Bellevue Washington, 1998.

Chapter VI - Choose Not to Mimic Leadership Personas

1. Cleary, T. *Zen Lessons: The Art of Leadership.* Shambhala Press, 1999.

2. Ledoux, L. "Synthesis of the Practice of Adaptive Leadership." Internet, 2009.

3. Bennis, W. *On Becoming a Leader.* Perseus Publishing, 1989.

4. Johansen, B. *Leaders Make the Future*. San Fransciso: Berrett-Koehler Publishers, 2009.

5. Lao Tao quote. *Brainy Quote.*

Bibliography of Influencers

In addition to experiences, every single idea in this book stands on the shoulders of many leadership writings.

Chapter I – What Most Leadership Conversations Gloss Over

Ambler, G. "6 Leadership Challenges Keeping Executives Awake." (Blog), 2013.

Ambler, G. "Leadership is Not a Title." (blog), 2016.

Barrett, R. *The New Leadership Paradigm*. Rutledge, 2010.

Cameron, K. *Diagnosing Organizational Culture*. San Francisco: Jossey-Bass Publishers, 2006.

Collins, J. *Good to Great: Why Some Companies Make the Leap and Others Don't*. Harper Collins Publishers, 2001.

Covey, S. *Seven Habits of Highly Successful People*. Schuster Inc. Publishing, 1989.

Deloitte Report, "Diversity and Inclusion." November 2015.

Dickson, G. and B. Tholl, *Bringing Leadership to Life in Health: LEADS in a Caring Environment*. Springer, 2014.

Drucker, P. "Managing Knowledge Means Managing Oneself." Essay. Drucker Foundation Letter, 2000.

Goleman, D., R. Buyatzis, and A. Mckee. *Primal Leadership: Unleashing the Power Emotional Intelligence*. Harvard Business Press, 2013.

Hall, B. *Values Shift: A Guide to Personal and Organization Transformation.* Resource Publications a Division of Twin Light Publishers, 2006.

Hartung, Adam. "Pursuing White Space Opportunity. White Paper." Industrial Research Institute, 2010.

Heifetz, R. "Adaptive Learning." *Healthcare Journal.* Vol. 38, No. 4,1995.

Hunt, V., D. Laxton and S. Prince. "Mckinsey & Company Report On Diversity." January 2015.

Knutson, L. "Integrative Leadership: An Embodied Practice." *Duke Health* (blog). 2017.

Kouzes, J., and B. Posner. *Credibility: How Leaders Gain It and Lose It, Why People Demand It*, 2011.

Learning and Transformation Blog. 2009.

MacLeod, H. "A Call for a New Connectivity." Healthcare Papers. Longwood Publishing: Vol.11, No.2, 2011.

MacLeod, H. "Creating a Complete Picture." Essay. Longwoods Publishing, 2014.

MacLeod, H. "A Last Word on the Balcony of Personal Reflection." Essay. Longwoods Publishing, 2015.

MacLeod, H. and A. Best. "Leadership White Space and Mindsets." Essay. Longwoods Publishing, 2015.

Quinn, R. *Deep Change: Discovering the Leader Within.* San Francisco: Jossey-Bass Publishers, 1996.

Ramos, I. "The Organizational Mind." Portugal: University of Minho, 2006.

MacLeod, H. and G. Low. "Organizational Connectivity." Essay. Reader Feedback. Longwoods Publishing, 2013.

Palsule, S., M. Chanvez. "Re-Humanizing Leadership." Dialogue Review, December 15, 2017.

Rummler, G. and A. Brache. *Improving Performance: How to Manage White Space on the Organizational Chart.* San Francisco: Jossey-Bass Publishers, 1995.

Schachter, H. "Five Management Traps That Waste Energy." The Globe and Mail, October 03, 2016.

Schein, E. *Organizational Culture and Leadership.* San Francisco: Jossey-Bass Publishers, 1992.

Taylor, M. and H. MacLeod. "Bridging the Leadership Gap." Essay. Longwoods Publishing, 2015.

Treasurer, B. "Leadership is Freakin Hard." (blog), 2015.

Tsao, A. "Humanistic Leadership: A New Era Has Begun." Blog, February 27, 2018.

Woodward, J. *Industrial Organizations: Theory and Practice.* New York: Dunellen, 1970.

Chapter II – Are Hearts, Spirits and Minds Important to You?

Axelrod, R. and H. MacLeod. "Engaging the Staff." Health Reform Journal. May/June 2002.

Ball, T. and G. Sekaly. "What's Changing: Discovering Shared Reality & Shared Vision. Managing Change." Winter 2006.

Ball, T. and H. MacLeod. "A Different Way of Thinking." Essay. Longwoods Publishing, 2013.

Eikenberg, D. "Why Soft Skills Are Harder." Forbes, July 12, 2018

Gentry, W., T. Weber, and G. Sadri. "Empathy in the Workplace." Center for Creative Leadership, 2007.

Gourguechon, P. "Empathy Is An Essential Leadership Skill And Theres Nothing Soft About It.' Forbes, December 26, 2017.

Heifetz, R. "Adaptive Learning." *Healthcare Journal.* Vol. 38, No. 4,1995.

Liopius, G. "Ways Inclusive Leadership Will Replace Diversity Initiatives." Forbes, July 31, 2017.

McCallum, J. "Followership: The Other Side Of Leadership." Ivey Business Journal, September-October 2013

MacLeod, H. "Working Together for Safe Efficient and Quality Care." Canadian Journal of Respiratory Therapy. Winter Vol. 46.4, 2010.

MacLeod, H. "Ghost of Healthcare Despair." Essay. Longwoods Publishing, 2012.

MacLeod, H. "Forging Complete Questions to Defeat the Ghost of Healthcare Despair." Essay. Longwoods Publishing, 2012.

MacLeod, H. "Soft Side Meets Hard Side." Essay. Longwoods Publishing, 2013.

MacLeod, H. and P. Scimeca-Davies. "Call Lights Are on—Are Care Givers Distracted?" Essay. Longwoods Publishing, 2013.

MacLeod, H., J. Shamian. "Do We Honour The Contributions Made By Our Most Precious Asset." Essay. Longwoods Publishing, 2013

MacLeod, H. and W. Nicklin. "Empathy Foundation for New Conversations." Essay. Long-woods Publishing, 2013.

MacLeod, H. "Surrounded by Opportunity." Essay. Longwoods Publishing, 2014.

Stewart, T. *Intellectual Capital – New Wealth for Organizations.* Doubleday, 1999.

Chapter III – Organizational Elasticity and Effectiveness

Covey, S. *Seven Habits of Highly Successful People.* Schuster Inc. Publishing, 1989.

Goleman, D., R. Buyatzis., and A. McKee. "Primal Leadership: Unleashing the Power of Emotional Intelligence." Harvard Business Press, 2013.

MacLeod, H. and J. Abbott. "Strategy and its Interplays." Essay. Longwoods Publishing, 2013.

MacLeod, H. and R. Alvarez "Four Mindsets." Essay. Longwoods Publishing, 2013.

MacLeod, H. and M. Davies. "Conditions Leaders Influence." Essay. Longwoods Publishing, 2013.

MacLeod, H. and G. Dickson. "Passive Following Versus Future Focused Leadership." Essay. Longwood Publishing, 2013.

Senge, P. *The Fifth Discipline: The Art & Practise of The Learning Organization.* Double Day Publishing, 1990.

Wheatley, M. *Finding Our Way. Leadership for an Uncertain Time.* San Francisco: Berrett-Koehler Publishers, 2005.

Yeo, A. Urban Balance Web Site Home Page, 2018.

Chapter IV – Paradox of Simultaneous Continuity and Change

Ball, T., S. Glouberman, and L. Verlaan-Cole. "Is Redesigning the Healthcare Systems a Complicated or Complex Challenge?" Blog Essay. October 2016.

Barr, S. "Peter Senge' Laws Of System Thinking." Pump Blog. 2014

Flood, R. *Rethinking the Fifth Discipline: Learning Within the Unknowable.* London: Routledge, 1999.

Dickon, G. and B. Tholl. "Bringing Leadership to Life in Health: LEADS in a Caring Environment." Springer, 2014.

Hall, S. *Wisdom: From Philosophy to Neuroscience.* New York: Alfred A. Knopf, 2010.

MacLeod, H. and M. Kirby. "Courage: A Rare Competency." Essay. Longwood Publishing, 2013

MacLeod, H. "Patient Experience." Essay. Longwoods Publishing, 2013.

Solovey, A. "Laws Of System Thinking In Software Development." Software Creating Mystery Blog, July 26, 2007.

Chapter V - Adaptive Action and Leadership

Heifetz, R. "Adaptive Learning." *Healthcare Journal.* Vol. 38, No. 4, 1995.

Heifetz, R. "Leadership Without Easy Answers." *Harvard University Press*, 1994.

Johnson, K. "The Lines Are Blurring: How Leaders Can Respond To The Ever Changing Work." Management Concepts, December 07, 2016.

MacLeod, H. and S. Lewis. "Asking the Unaskable, Thinking the Unthinkable." Longwoods Publishing, *Healthcare Quarterly.* 15 (1) 2012.

MacLeod, H. "Overcoming Mental Models of Traditional Healthcare Leadership." Managing Change, 2013.

MacLeod, H. and L. Thompson. "If We Had a Magic Wand." Essay. Longwoods Publishing, 2014.

Macleod, H. and A. Best. "Leadership White Space and Mindsets." Essay. Longwoods Publishing, 2015.

Martin, D. "Dear Class Of 2020." Open Letter Series on Leadership and Transformation. Longwoods Publishing, 2017.

Pop, O. "How To Embrace These 4 Leadership Paradoxes."Hype Innovation Blog. November 23, 2016.

Saul, J. and A. Best. "Guiding Principles and a New Mindset." Essay. Longwoods Publishing, 2013.

Swimme, B. and M. Tucker. *Journey of the Universe.* Yale University Press, 2011.

Vor, T. *Leadership Blog.* 2016

Chapter VI - Choose Not to Mimic Leadership Personas

MacLeod, H. "Overcoming the Mental Models of Traditional Healthcare Leadership." Managing Change. Summer, 2003

MacLeod, H. "Stop Tiptoeing Around What Matters." Longwoods Publishing, 2013.

MacLeod, H. and S. Jarvis. "Winds of Change and Growing Storms." Essay. Longwoods Publishing, 2013.

MacLeod, H. "A Last Word from the Balcony of Personal Reflection." Essay. Longwoods Publishing, 2015.

Piper, W. "The Little Engine That Could." Dunlap, 2001.

Sudanshu, P., M. Chavez. "Classics: Re-Humanizing Leadership." Dialogue Review, December 15, 2017.

ACKNOWLEDGEMENTS

I have been truly blessed by the support of extraordinary people who provided me with counsel and opportunities to grow as a leader and to learn from setbacks. I have been able to explore a wide range of personal and work experiences, and in the process, I learned from a rich mosaic of people. I was fortunate to have co-authors write with me on over one hundred essays and articles about leadership and change. The support, dialogue, and freedom to experiment with colleagues influenced the creation of this book.

Thank you ... John Abbott, Richard Alverez, Mary Atkinson, Richard, Axelrod, Carolyn Baker, Ted Ball, Rachel Bard, Tanya Barnett, Marsha Barnes, Dr. Robert Bell, Dr. Alan Best (PhD), Briana Broderick, Karen Cardiff, Dr. Brendan Carr, Dr. Doug Cochrane, Peter Cox, Tom Closson, Janet Davidson, Maura Davies, Paula Davies-Scimeca, Ken Deane, Dr. Dirk F. de Korne, Dr. Graham Dickson (PhD), Dr. Mary Ditton, Dr. Diane Finegood (PhD), Don Ford, Sara Givens, Dr. David Goldstein, Brie Gowan, Kelly Grimes, Dr. Chris Hayes, Andrew Holt, Dr. Alan Hudson, Sheila Jarvis, Bart Johnson, Vickie Kaminski, Dr. Gillian Kernaghan , Michael Kirby , Dr. Jack Kitts, Sarah Kramer ,Carol Kushner, Steven Lewis, Dr. Ron Lindstrom (PhD), Dr. Charles Low, Dr. Graham Lowe (PhD), Dr. Marilyn MacDonald (PhD), Gail MacKean, Murray Martin, James Mastin, Marg McAlister, Lindsay McGee, Dr. Adrienne Melck, Dr. Elizabeth Meuser (PhD), Dr. Tina Montemurro, Wendy Nicklin, Kevin Noel, Chris Power, Dr. Jessie Saul (PhD), Dr. Judith Shamian, (PhD), Shirlee Sharkey, Lisa Shiozaki, Dr. Sam Sheps, Louise Simard, Kavita Singh, Dr. Kevin Smith, Dr. Anne Snowdon (PhD), Dr. Kim Spears (PhD), Dr. Denise Stockley (PhD), Dr. Marilyn Taylor (PhD), Dr. Joshua Tepper, Leslee Thompson, Joanne Trypuc, Tom Van Dawark, Sue VanderBent, Marlene van Dijk, and Martin Vogel

I was also humbled by the willingness of people who provided me feedback on the essays and articles. Your struggles, comments, and opinions influenced the writing of this book.

To my critical readers, who invested countless hours reading my drafts and providing honest feedback on how this book could be improved, thank you: Harpreet Bassi, Alex Berland, Graham Dickson, Dr. Chris Eagle, Kelly Grimes, Ron Lindstrom, Wendy Nicklin, Roger Parsonage, Don Phillippon, and Katie White.

I am particularly indebted to my son Marc. You knew what I wanted to say and helped me say it better. You helped me stay on message and keep the concept of "how reflection fuels, people matter, and relationships make the difference," the connecting thread throughout the book. To my son Scott, your passion for everything in life is an inspiration.

To my late mother, Katherine, and grandfather John Macleod, you both validated me as a person, provided feedback that built me up instead of knocking me down, reduced my fear, and affirmed my importance, presence, and role in our family system.

While I, Hugh MacLeod, authored this book, describing my role as such is an overstatement. Without the significant support from Linda, my best friend since high school and my life partner, the idea for this book would still be sitting on a shelf. Your love and support is impossible to measure.

SUMMARY NOTES - READERS GUIDE

Why I Wrote This Book

"From my experience, few people are burdened by self-awareness. When I held up a mirror to my people interactions I realized something: Who is always there? It's me, and I noticed myself engaging in relationship patterns over and over again, with different people." What is your story?

How to Use This Book

"This book requires reader participation. The weight of the message is within the reader, not on the pages. Words and ideas shared in this book are by no means universal truths. They are personal experiences and understandings that are open to adaptation. Use the personal insights as a springboard for self-discovery. Note the pages or insights that encourage your self-reflection. Mark the lines or sections that challenge your views. Revisit these inclinations at a later date to determine whether their weight or significance is lasting." How is your leadership journey connected with your interior self?

My Experiences

"I had the privilege of experiencing many organizational environments: retail sales; ownership of a small business; human-resource-management services in the insurance, utility, and healthcare sectors; labour negotiations; board governance; learner engagement at various universities; local and provincial healthcare administration; government service; provincial climate-change planning; and national quality and safety improvement. I spent time in all organizational spaces; front-line worker, middle manager, senior executive, and chief operating officer. In the process, I gained an appreciation of the dynamics that take place between people and relationships within and between organizational spaces. I am eternally grateful for the multitude of individuals who graciously shared their time, words, wisdom, and encouragement along my leadership journey. Often, these individuals had confidence in me before I

had confidence in my own ability. These individuals provided me with the essential space and pivotal opportunities to grow." How would you write your story?

Chapter 1 - What Most Leadership Conversations Gloss Over

Leadership is Personal

"What makes leadership personal and hard work isn't the theoretical; it's the practical. It's not about knowing what to say or do. It's about whether you're willing to experience the discomfort, risk, and uncertainty of saying or doing it. To quote Aristotle, "To avoid discomfort, say nothing, do nothing, be nothing. How are you experiencing leadership discomfort, risk and uncertainty?

Define Your Leadership

"As leadership is personal and unique to the individual, creating and cultivating your own personal definition provides an anchor for your role as leader. Your definition of leadership affects how you think about your role, how you act, your relationship with others, and ultimately, your results." How is your leadership brand a work in progress; changing and evolving as you move through your life and career?

Leadership Cannot Be Imposed

"Real-world experiences create real-world leadership. Without experience, we run the risk of creating leadership theorists versus leaders. Leadership is learned through trial and error, through mucking it up and making mistakes and having the gumption to learn from what worked and did not work. Unfortunately, in our instant-microwave culture, we want to be leaders now!" What words would you use to describe "learning"? Is it easier to experience learning when things are good?

Personal Leadership Traps

"Over the years, I witnessed and contributed to the following costly leadership traps: experience; winners; agreement; communication and macro-management." What leadership traps are holding you hostage?

Human Hard Drives and Blind Spots

"Our 'human hard drives' have been shaped, and continue to be shaped, by our perspectives, perceptions, reactions, and expectations. As our human hard drive swells with personal insights and understandings, we develop various coping mechanisms, biases, and habits to protect them (firewalls, anti-virus 'software' and security 'programs'). It is essential to pay attention to your hard drive and blind spots." Up and down the corporate ladder, how do people respond when you approach them?

Truths and Untruths

"To combat self-delusion and become more self-aware, each of us as leaders need to first acknowledge our potential for self-delusion and become conscious of our world views, assumptions, and mental models, then rigorously challenge them to root out delusional notions." What are your leadership truths and untruths?

Organizational Space Conditions

"Every individual has the capacity to contribute to organizational growth. Individuals carry the seeds of success: skills, talents, potentialities, and enthusiasm. Unfortunately, for many those same seeds contain too many intellectual, emotional, and systemic barriers. Liberating the "bottoms" and integrating the "middles" is how learning organizations succeed." Think about your organization. How healthy is your middle-management and front-line organizational space? What's your contribution?

Organizational White Space

"The 'organizational chart map' is essentially an aggregate of isolated power blocks with a steep hierarchy command center. Organizational static box images imply

rigid turf boundaries, drawn with black boxes and lines on blank white paper, whereas high-performing organizations draw out the dynamic and fluid white space between all the lines and organizational boxes.Two portraits: People are torn between multiple and ever-changing priorities and people are self-directed and multi-skilled." What portrait best captures your organization or the department that you have responsibility for? What's your contribution to the portrait? What needs to change?

Everyone Wants to Change and No One Wants to Change
Many of us are armchair voyeurs of leadership and change rather than the players in it. As we indulge in our "fantasy" change games (endless meetings, symposia, and conferences), it sometimes feels like we are trying to convince ourselves that we are involved "It's self-awareness that triggers your desire for change. It's self-awareness that keeps you growing. It's an interesting paradox: I learn more about myself so I can focus better on others. And by focusing on the development of others, high-performing environments are created in which people feel safe, take on more risk, and grow in the process." Are you asking this question continually: How can I create a culture that encourages the expression of intelligence, passion, commitment, and experience by people at all levels of the organization?

Chapter II - Are Hearts, Spirits and Minds Important to You?

People "Are" Our Greatest Asset
"We find the 'people are our greatest asset' concept within the frame of value statements that include words such as 'respect,' 'trust,' 'diversity,' and 'openness,' Far too often, this is merely wallpaper within a picture frame, with no commitment to alter the organizational mindset." Can you provide examples of what your organization does to give all employees the feeling that they are the most important assets? As a leader, how do you ensure the people asset gets as much management time discussion as the fiscal assets?

Soft Impacts Hard

"Simply put, it is soft things like organizational culture, teachable moments, effective collaboration, ability to experience change, and learning that creates friction with hard things like consumer satisfaction, crisis frequency, retention of staff, cost of performance, cost of service, share holder value, and profit." What stage of soft impacts hard learning are you at? Where do you want to be? What's stopping you?

Empathy a People Matter Foundation

"Empathy is the ability to experience and relate to the thoughts, emotions, or experiences of others. To be drawn to leadership work is to be drawn to the center of the human condition—the eye of the storm. Leaders who are committed to change, but are without in-depth learning, are at risk of confusing the power of the organization with their own strength. Empathy is demonstrated by listening with curiosity and compassion." How is your leadership signalling that you are part of the conversation to understand?

Leveraging and Connecting Values, Principles, and Ethics

"Value principles and ethics guide the development of relationship patterns. We need to understand our values and the values held by those we work with. For any form of transformation to occur within an organization, and (more specifically) in order for it to flourish, a great measure of mindfulness must be placed upon the diversity of people that make up the organization." Values determine the ethics we form and use to guide our lives. How do you practice your values and ethics to form the morals that prompt your decisions?

Diversity of Thinking and Inclusion

"An organization's commitment to diversity is visible through the manner in which it creates and maintains its culture. The manner in which individual members are viewed and treated projects the character of the organization and its collective leadership." As a leader, how do you demonstrate dignity, respect, and worth as paramount to communicating corporate commitment to diversity?

Culture Eats Strategy for Breakfast

"Understanding the dynamics of culture is important for everyone and essential for leaders. Culture originates from three primary sources: beliefs, values, and assumptions of the founders of organizations; learning experiences of group members as their organization evolves; and new beliefs, values, and assumptions brought in by new members and leaders. To a large extent, organizational culture is shaped and maintained by leaders as they set the stage for expected behaviour." How are you setting the stage?

Chapter III - Organizational Elasticity and Effectiveness

Multi-dimensional Relationships and External Conditions

"The genetic code of an organization is embedded in thousands of people interactions that occur every day between people. We are aware that structure follows strategy, and that function precedes form. We have also witnessed that relationships run the show, and without relationships, there is no strategy implementation; there is no function to begin with." In your organization are employees unclear of the present they find themselves in and do they fear the future ahead? What's your role?

Going to the Dance Floor

"What would happen if we spent a significant part of our time being engaged in the space where services are actually delivered? Some organizations, especially those adopting lean management systems, are doing this and finding it dramatically changes their understanding of how human systems work and what needs to change. It also puts the power and responsibility for continuous improvement in the hands of those who actually deliver services. Organizations have a soul, a spirit, something that is outside of your organizational structure and systems." How are you tapping the organizational soul and spirit?

Circles of Connectivity and Patterns of Energy

"If leadership requires followship, is leadership a shift from managing others to managing yourself with others? Is leadership operating from the inside out through the observations of the motives, intentions, feelings, judgments, and attributes that drive our responses to others?" We know that people are capable of brilliance. The answers to the dilemmas we face are within our own organizations. How are you discovering what gets in the way?

Personal Insights from Home

"As leaders, we have very little direct control over how other people think, but if there's something about the environment a person is in that creates either more or less meaning in their work, then leaders are on the hook for something different." How do you pay attention to organizational environmental conditions?

Mindsets

"Forward-thinking organizations are preparing for what the next few years will throw at them, and leadership is often touted as what will help weather the storm. This logic is not wrong; in fact, it's right. However, leadership doesn't depend on a few skills or even many skills. Leadership is more than a skill, it's a mindset that shapes everything we do. Organizations recognize a need to adjust underlying mindsets, but often they are reluctant to address the root causes of why leaders act the way they do." How do you identify some of the deepest "below the surface" thoughts, feelings, assumptions, and beliefs as a precondition of behavioural change?

Competing Will and Damaging Mindsets

"The following story is a metaphor for competing will and mindsets. One evening, an elder told his grandson about a battle that goes on inside people between two wolves that are inside of us all. One wolf is full of anger, envy, jealousy, sorrow, regret, greed, arrogance, self-pity, guilt, resentment, inferiority, lies, false pride, superiority, and false ego. The other wolf is filled with joy, peace, love, hope, serenity, humility, kindness, benevolence, empathy, generosity, truth, compassion, and faith. The grandson thought about it for a minute, and then asked his grandfather,

"Which wolf wins?" The grandfather simply replied, "The one that you feed." What wolf gets rewarded and fed in your organization? What wolf do you feed?

Mindset Shift
"We must fight the normal tendency to pull inward. Leadership is about: creating opportunities for people to understand the dangers and opportunities for the organization; fostering broad participation that quickly identifies problems and solutions; sparking innovative and creative thinking and solutions by encouraging different points of view; encouraging collaboration throughout the organization, ensuring that people are connected not only to each other but to the issues as well; and ensuring implementation with accountability by letting people know they have the freedom to carry out the agreed upon plan." What's your role?

Liberation and Authenticity
"Ultimately, our influence does not stem from the titles we are given or the marching orders we cast. Our influence stems from our liberation—liberation from self-prominence and the trickery of being all-knowing. Influence is earned through our ability to harness the energy and competencies of our people. The overall success of an organization is not established by the completion of tasks or agendas laid forth, but through the dedication of its members." As a leader how are you creating levels of devotion founded on, and fluctuated by, feelings of inclusion and recognition, the ability to contribute, and the opportunity for growth?

Chapter IV - Paradox of Simultaneous Continuity and Change

Systemic, Practical and Personal Contradictions
"Managing contradictions and complexity requires managing within the paradoxical nature of all inter-connection, and participation is a leadership competency requirement. To suspend the temptation to resolve paradox is difficult for leaders. As we become increasingly aware of all aspects, visible and obscure, of organizational life, comprehending contradictions and complexity can offer some of the

most important learning in our lives." Many leaders have been schooled in a model of rationality and linear thinking about causality. What have you learned about managing contradictions and complexity?

Differentiating Complicated and Complex Scenarios
"The degree of inter-connectedness between the individual parts of a system helps to differentiate complicated and complex scenarios. Challenges that appear to be simple early on may be regarded as complicated when more is known about the challenge. We need to refrain from making assumptions early in the process. We must gain a full understanding of the circumstances and variables at hand before a prognosis is determined. Often, we apply simple solutions to complex challenges. We are surprised to only scratch the surface of the challenge at hand." How often do you fail to understand simple, complicated, and complex problems, why?

Experiencing Complexity First Hand
"Science has shown us again and again that our reality consists of ecologies, systems, and networks, yet our preference for compartmentalized thinking persists in breaking problems down in ways that refuse to see larger interrelationships. Looking only at the domains that we've arranged neatly in silos, we fall victim to the law of unintended consequences. We are a society that loves piecemeal approaches in many respects." How do you reshape your thinking to benefit from a broader perspective while still moving forward and taking action?

Complexity to the Rescue
"Most so-called problems in the organizational systems are not problems at all. What we face are paradoxes created in the context of what should be anticipated characteristics and behaviours of complex adaptive systems. We need to learn this distinction. We need to stop trying to extract simple nuances from complex problems." What are you learning?

Leaders Contribute to Complexity

"We can work to simplify processes and recognize patterns, but we must be aware that patterns do not necessarily repeat in the exact same way. The paradox of continuity and change is continually operative. Crisis and opportunity are inseparable. In a crisis, there is an opportunity for change but not a guarantee. In opportunity there is a possibility for stasis or change but no guarantee for one or the other. Understanding the paradoxical nature of organizations prepares leaders to handle complicated and complex processes." How are you developing your understanding that organizational problems are simple and complicated, at the same time? How are you avoiding cookie-cutter approaches?

Asking the Unaskable and Thinking the Unthinkable

"Asking "why" questions of self and others break the ritual conversations that take place. The key is in framing of the question: the timing of the asking, in a manner that creates commitment to continuously learn. The listening side of the question asked is listening to hear, to understand, versus listening to counter." Do you ask this key "why" question: Have I tolerated behaviour in myself and in others that conflicts with a commitment to the values, purpose and vision of my organization?

How Well Do You Ask

"How well do you ask questions? The 'ability to ask questions' doesn't usually show up on any list of leadership competencies or job description requirements. However, asking effective questions is a major component of any leader's job, and asking the proper questions often distinguishes outstanding leaders from average ones (or worse, poor ones)." Are you involved in discourse consisting primarily of polite banter or debate that falls short of naming conflict? What is your contribution?

When Assumptions Trounce Truth

"I know you just heard us laughing and cracking a joke in the hall. I get it. You don't see anything funny with your mom confined to that bed, attached to all those monitors. I understand. I do. Please understand that while you were waiting

outside we saved the young woman next door. She couldn't breathe. Now she can. We didn't think we'd get a breathing tube down in time. We also restarted the heart of the man across the hall. We were unsure if his heart would restart, but it did. The patient next door to him wasn't so lucky. We tried. I begged God, but she went anyway. Think about a recent event/meeting that you were in. Did your personal assumptions accurately reflect the current realities?

How Far Can You See

"As we move into the high-velocity context of the 21st-century economy, leaders will need to be open to a future not yet created. In that sense, our own future is a blank canvas. Leverage lies in understanding dynamic complexity and seeing inter-relationships rather than linear cause-and-effect chains. Leaders must master an ability to remain relevant in today's fast-paced and exponentially changing world." Do you look beyond what's in front of you, especially when daily tasks take up so much time and energy? How do you become future-oriented and still handle day-to-day challenges?

Chapter V - Adaptive Action and Leadership

Problems and Paradoxes

"Let's use the metaphor of "on the balcony of personal reflection" above the "dance floor" to depict what it means to gain the distanced perspective we need to see what is really happening. If we stay moving on the dance floor, all we will see will be the people dancing with and around us. If we move up to the balcony, we may see a very different picture. When we move back and forth between balcony and dance floor, we can continually assess what is happening in our organization and take corrective midcourse action. If we perfect this skill, we might even be able to do both simultaneously, keeping one eye on the events happening around us and the other eye on the larger patterns and dynamics." What are you doing to develop this skill?

Inter-Connected Adaptive Activities and Action

"Adaptive leadership takes you out of your daily routine to unknown territory requiring ways of acting that are outside your repertoire, with no guarantee of your competence or your success. There is a bit of paradox here. On one hand, you are trying to lead on behalf of something you believe in that is beyond your individual interest. On the other hand, in order to be most effective in doing so, you need to pay attention to how you manage, use, and deploy yourself. It is not about self-indulgence, it is about smart personal leadership." How are you developing adaptive leadership skills?

Rational, Formative and Transformative Approaches to Change

"As players are choosing for themselves alone within the play action, another paradox inheres. Every player is simultaneously in a process of continuity and change, as are the teams, coaches, spectators and game. The whole is not greater than the sum of its parts; the whole is different from the sum of its parts." Those who believe in control and prediction will think and act in very different ways from those who believe that the future is unknown, and thus, unpredictable. What do you believe?

Resiliency

"Every day organizational work is subject to changing conditions. Resilience acknowledges the dynamic nature of this work much like the dynamics of a hockey game, and the intrinsic capacity of an organization, its component parts, and its people to adjust prior to, during and after dynamic disturbances to maintain required operations under both expected and unexpected conditions. Resiliency is the ability to persevere when difficulties arise. Resilient leaders are persistent and able to cope with the setbacks." Do you learn from your mistakes and bounce back?

Blurring Lines and Competing Tensions

"Leaders in the midst of adaptive change must be able to artfully guide their people through a balance of disorientation and new learning. They need to hold the group in an optimal state of tension and disequilibrium that stimulates a quest for

learning, without jarring people so much that they simply are not able to learn." How do you hold and lead a group in an optimal tension state?

Change Principles

"*There are several placements on which you can find yourself on the face of a transformation-change wave. If you are too far ahead, the wave will crash down and you will be at the mercy of its violent surge. If you are tentative and fail to harness the available energy, you run the risk of being left behind. If you place yourself in perfect trim and continue to make adjustments, you can actually ride the wave.*" What is it that you are doing that allows you to become one with the wave?

Renewal

"*To continue to evolve as leaders, we must truly embrace the areas where we're naturally less confident and comfortable. We must model this self-awareness for those we lead. A leaders journey is a series of trapeze bars that we seize and swing from progressively, grabbing the next bar just after we let go of the previous.*" What are you doing between the bars to experience the most learning?

Chapter VI - Chose Not to Mimic Leadership Personas

Blossom the Leader Within

"*Think about it. Why are you a leader? Are you ever really prepared? Why should people follow you? Start by paying attention to how you work, not just what you know or what you accomplish. How do you learn? How do you share information, make decisions, and influence others? How do you build and nurture relationships?*" Are you paying attention to these questions to gain insight?

Future Focussed Leadership

"Private and public businesses face a virtually unprecedented variety of challenges, from harvesting profits in mature economies with flat or declining growth, to establishing toeholds in emerging countries, to creating the next wave of disruptive innovation, to working through the complexity of changing regulation, and everything in between. Each of these unique challenges requires a unique kind of leader. One size does not fit all. There is an abundance of brilliant minds, brave souls, compassionate hearts, technological wizards, and creative geniuses amongst us. Stale protocols, outmoded agendas, incomplete strategies, forceful top-down mandates, self-serving ambitions, and unavailing quick fixes must be abandoned." What leadership role can you play?

My Personal Journey and Truths

"The Chinese philosopher Lao Tao said, 'When I let go of what I am, I become what I might be.' Every road and intersection I chose presented a choice, and following a road never travelled before was a journey. On my personal leadership-learning journey, there were long and short roads, smooth and rocky roads, crooked and straight paths." What I see depends on what I am prepared to see. I believe reflection fuels, people matter, and relationships make the difference. Do you? Are you "Humanizing Your Leadership"?